This book belongs to

Tuck

Training Your Own
HORSE

Training Your Own
HORSE

Mary Rose FBHS

Author of
The Horsemaster's Notebook

Harrap London

First published in Great Britain 1977
by GEORGE G. HARRAP & CO. LTD
182–184 High Holborn, London WC1V 7AX

© *Mary Rose* 1977

ISBN 0 245 53151 3

Printed in Great Britain by offset lithography by
Billing & Sons Limited, Guildford, London, and Worcester

To all my students, equine and human, past, present and future, with many thanks for all you have taught me so far

Preface

This book has been written not so much for the backyard horse owner, but more to fulfil a need which has become apparent to me over the past few years. There are so many young people today who take a few months' training course followed by an examination and then set out on a career in the horse industry. Some work under qualified trainers and instructors, but many are forced to work on their own and they know only too well that they have hardly begun to scratch the surface of the knowledge that they need for their chosen profession. It is primarily to these young instructor/trainers that I am addressing this book, but I hope that it may also be helpful and stimulating to more experienced riders who aspire towards training their own horse.

MARY ROSE
Colorado, May 1976

Acknowledgements

The line drawings and diagrams are by Dave Steckelburg, Anne Scully and others. The photographs (between pages 46–47 and pages 158–159) were taken by the author unless individually specified.

Contents

1 *First Things First*

Selecting a horse

Selecting a horse is very much a matter of individual, personal preference. Probably, only a very few people will deliberately set out to buy a horse with a specific, single purpose in mind. Most people want their horse to be a pleasure animal, capable of competing in local shows, taking part in Riding Club or Pony Club Events, perhaps capable of making a good hunter, and almost certainly, a pleasant hack. There is certainly no reason why the same horse should not be able to do all these things, provided you ride well enough to train your horse beyond the elementary stage of plain usefulness, and the purpose of this book is to offer practical guidance on how to achieve your ends.

Today's horse shows, dressage competitions, hunter trials and three-phase events require the horse and rider to present a picture of ease and elegance. There is as much emphasis on the extended paces as on the highly collected ones, even in the dressage arena. The horse must have that elusive quality, *presence*, in order to awake and hold the judge's interest. His bearing should be that of a high-couraged animal, generous, energetic and free-going, yet calm and confident, light and obedient. It is hardly surprising, therefore, that there are so many thoroughbred horses at the top in every sphere of horse activity. However, the honours are certainly not exclusively held by thoroughbred horses, and many people will choose horses from among the other breeds.

Temperament

Whatever the breed of horse or pony that you choose, there are certain basic principles you would do well to remember. In the first place, you should choose a horse with a good temperament. You may be surprised that I place temperament at the top of my list, but, in my opinion, it is actually easier to overcome, by training, a fault in conformation, given a good temperament, than it is to overcome a bad temperament, however superb the conformation. A horse should be generous, willing and kind; full of courage, power and gaiety, and above all, you should like your horse.

I hope you will give temperament a very high place on your list of priorities, whether you are setting out to buy a horse, or are thinking of breeding your own. When I am considering breeding a mare of my own I always try to visit the stallions I have short-listed as possible suitable mates by reason of their pedigrees or performance. I like to check the horse out for myself, watch how he is handled and how he behaves, and take a look at some of his young stock—not only to see how he reproduces himself in regard to conformation, but particularly to see what kind of temperament he passes on.

Conformation

Good conformation is certainly an important consideration in selecting a horse, either to buy or to breed from. Faults in conformation often point out to us in advance possible weaknesses in a horse and warn us that he will not stand up to the stress of training and hard work. For example, an upright shoulder and short, upright pasterns not only signify that the horse will be a less comfortable ride than one with a long sloping shoulder, but also that the very important shock-absorbing mechanism of his front end is not as good as it should be and he may later suffer from any of the lamenesses associated with concussion.

When evaluating a horse's conformation, bear in mind that make and shape differs slightly in the different breeds of horse, and you should make your comparison against the best available specimen of the breed you are considering, and not automatically compare every horse you see with the thoroughbred. Remember, also, that faulty riding and training can develop the wrong muscles in a horse. His total shape can be changed by correct work, which will put him in the proper shape, i.e. rounded, with head down, quarters under him, back supple, and with the right muscles developed.

Broadly speaking, there are certain desirable characteristics to look for in the conformation of any riding horse. His head should be attractive and not too large, the forehead should be broad, the eye large and confident, the nose fine and the nostrils wide open. The neck should be long and well set-on, it should be fairly light so that it can be easily suppled and bent. The shoulders should be long and sloping and the withers prominent, well shaped, and reaching far back into a short, strong back. The hindquarters should be long and broad. The horse should appear fairly close to the ground, not too long in the leg, and the knees should be broad and flat, the forearm comparatively long and the cannon bone fairly short. The hind leg should be fairly straight, with long, well muscled thighs and large hocks. The pasterns should be quite long and sloping, the feet well shaped and appropriate in size to the horse. The 'bottom line' of the horse should appear longer than the 'top line', which will be so, if the shoulder has a good slope. The skin should be fine and silky, the muscles well defined and hard. The horse should carry his head and tail proudly and should move freely and straight, with long, regular strides.

You will be most unlikely to find all these good points in the same animal and you certainly should not expect to find 'the perfect horse'. But if a horse has most of these good points of conformation, a good temperament and also shows 'quality' he is probably a good one.

Action

The third general principle to bear in mind is good action. If his conformation is good, the horse is likely to move well. Generally, a good walker will move well in his other paces, so pay attention to the walk. It should be long and swinging, with active, rhythmic strides. The horse should move straight, and it is more important that he should be good looking when moving than a perfect picture standing still. Watch the horse trot straight towards you and straight away from you, as well as observing him from the side. He should move straight, with roomy, unhurried strides and good rhythm, his joints should be supple and he should step well under his body with his hind feet, taking an equal length stride with each hind leg.

Soundness

Soundness is also a very important consideration in choosing a horse. A young horse with good conformation will probably be a sound horse, provided he has not been subjected to over strenuous training or racing as a two-year-old. Unfortunately, it is very difficult to find a thoroughbred horse who has not been raced as a two-year-old, and sometimes they have been raced very hard. A horse at two is very immature and his body is hardly capable of withstanding the strain of training or racing without suffering some ill effects.

In selecting breeding stock, soundness is no less important. It is most unwise to breed from a mare who is unsound in any way. That may sound rather harsh, if you have been planning to breed from your wonderful hunter mare who sprained her tendons last season. But consider the fact that possibly it was some weakness in her conformation that caused her to break down in the first place, and by breeding from her, you may pass this weakness on to the foal. It is a little more difficult to evaluate the meaning of some injury in the stallion you are planning to breed to. You have to decide whether, if he has splints, for instance, or suffered bowed tendons or something similar, he sustained the injury because of some shortcoming in his conformation, or whether it was caused by over-strenuous training at too early an age.

Let us hope, however, that you have been able to find that rare gem, an unspoilt three-year-old who has good temperament, good conformation and action and is sound. He has not been raced and is unbroken, but has, hopefully, been well and quietly handled by his breeder since birth. How the horse turns out in the end is going to depend on how you set about his training now. There are, unfortunately, many badly trained and spoiled horses and ponies in the world, and the reason is nearly always that their early training has been hurried—particularly in the case of a young horse showing promise. Taking a horse into competition too early, whether as a show horse, a dressage horse, or a jumper, or taking him hunting before he has had a really thorough basic training, is always a temptation. But it is seldom possible to make up later what has been omitted at the beginning, so try to remember to say to yourself over and over, when training a horse—'I have plenty of time'. We live in an age of instant action, but the horse has not changed, and it still takes a long time for him to develop, both physically and mentally, and to understand what you want from him.

The horse's nature

In many ways horses have not changed much despite their thousands of years of association with man. They are gregarious, nervous, highly strung animals with very acute senses and quick reactions. They have very strong instincts, and fear is one of the strongest. Horses have little reasoning power, but very good memories, particularly of facts, places, other horses, and anyone or anything that has frightened them in the past. In training horses, therefore, we develop in them the habit of obedience by the association of ideas. The right response is liberally rewarded, with a word, a pat or a titbit, to associate obedience with pleasure in the horse's mind. These associations must be perfectly clear and we must be quite certain that the horse knows what we want. It is vital for the trainer to be in sympathy with the horse, to know his feelings and to anticipate his evasions. Only then can he be certain if some disobedience is the result of fright, misunderstanding or naughtiness. In any case, the trainer should aim at making the habit of obedience so automatic in the horse that eventually it becomes second nature to him.

Qualities of a good horse trainer

Just as there are certain basic qualities which we look for in a young horse, so there are certain basic essentials to look for in a good trainer—whether you are thinking of training your horse yourself, or employing the services of a professional. It requires knowledge, patience, sympathy and skill to train a horse properly. The trainer must be quiet and tactful, but also determined, and he or she must have plenty of self-control and self-confidence. The trainer must understand the horse thoroughly, and know how his mind and body works, so that he can be certain that the horse is capable, both mentally and physically, of doing what is asked.

The mind of the horse

To understand the mind of the horse, we must remember that, in their wild state, horses survived by the development of very acute senses and quick reactions. Even after so many years of domestication, the young horse still reacts instinctively to anything which frightens him, by wheeling round, kicking, bucking or running away.

All horses enjoy company, particularly the company of other horses, and they will imitate each other. This fact can certainly be used to advantage in the training of a horse, by using an old, steady horse as a school master. But, on the other hand, the young horse will pay more attention to his trainer if he is away from other horses.

Early handling

In training horses, we aim to produce a state of complete and automatic obedience, combined with full mental and physical development. The first thing we have to do, therefore, is to overcome the horse's natural fear and gain his confidence. Handling the young horse yourself, grooming him, feeding him, and generally getting to know him, is all part of his training.

Always approach young horses quietly and without fear. Speak before moving and move slowly and quietly. Actual lessons, for example, teaching the horse to lead, must be kept very short at first. It is better to give a young horse three ten minute sessions a day than one lesson of half an hour.

The everyday treatment of the young horse, whether he is turned out in a field, in his stable, or during his work, is of the utmost importance. It is now that his lifelong habits are formed, and if we treat him always with friendliness, quiet determination and complete fearlessness, it will develop in him such a confidence in people that he is very unlikely ever to get bad habits such as kicking or biting.

Henry Wynmalen, in a statement regarding the everyday treatment of young horses, in his book *Dressage* says: 'It is never necessary to hit a horse; it is a sin to do so in his stable; and it is quite unpardonable to do so at his head.' To me, this sentence ranks high among the little gems I would like to see written in block capitals and pinned to every stable wall. Another such, thought, is: THINK. It is so terribly easy to make a horse head-shy and difficult to bridle, groom and clip, and it may take years to regain his confidence after someone hits him about the head.

Our ability to train horses depends on the establishment of our mental ascendancy over them. To resort to thoughtless, irrational and possibly cruel behaviour ourselves, is to relinquish our claim to mental ascendancy, since such actions are the result of fear and lack of confidence in ourselves, and the horse knows it. This is not to say that proper correction has no place in the horse's training, but we will discuss such correction in detail later on.

Use of the voice

The horse is, by nature, a very gentle creature. His hearing is acute and he is very sensitive to the human voice. Right from the start we should use the voice quietly, to encourage our young horse and give him confidence. It is certainly not necessary to shout at him. If correction is necessary at this stage, a very slightly raised voice will be quite sufficient.

It is worth remembering that if things go wrong you should be quick to blame yourself, rather than your horse. Quite probably you have tried to teach him too much, too quickly, or he has failed to understand what you want due to muddled aids. Try to have everything working in favour of success whenever you teach the horse anything. For example, it is just as easy to start off teaching him to lead going towards his friends as it is to try going the other way, and the horse will obey much more readily. Teach every new lesson when the horse is in a quiet, obedient frame of mind, but don't work him till he is so tired first that he can't assimilate the lesson.

Lightness of aids

If, in the end, we want the horse to answer the finest, lightest aid, it makes sense to employ, right from the start, only the lightest aid. It is just as easy to teach a young horse to move over in his loose box from a light pressure of the hand, as it is from a hefty slap, and it will start our horse out in the right direction if we treat him always quietly and gently but with confidence, firmness and common sense.

The illustrations on pages 8 to 24 are all concerned with various aspects of confirmation.

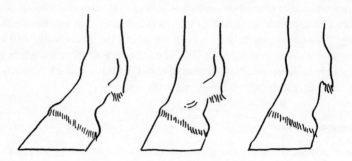

(LEFT)   Normal angulation of hoop and pastern
(MIDDLE)   A short upright pastern predisposing to injuries of the fetlock joint, ringbone of the pastern joint, and to navicular bursitis
(RIGHT)   Long upright pastern predisposes to injuries of the fetlock joint and navicular bursa

Long upright pastern with a broken foot and pastern axis caused by lowering of the heels in an attempt to produce normal angulation of the hoof wall

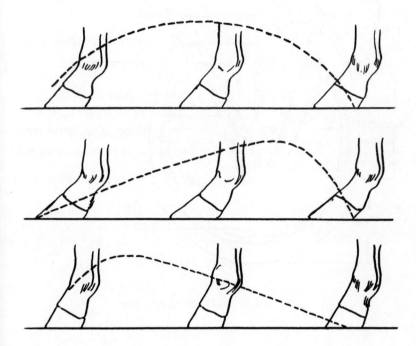

Conformation and its effect on action

(TOP)   Flight of a foot with normal foot and pastern axis. The peak of the arc occurs as the foot passes the opposite supporting foot

(MIDDLE)   Flight of a foot with foot and pastern axis less than normal: long toe; low heel. The peak of the arc occurs before the foot reaches the opposite supporting foot

(BOTTOM)   Flight of the foot with foot axis greater than normal: short toe, high heel. The peak of the arc occurs after the foot passes the opposite supporting foot

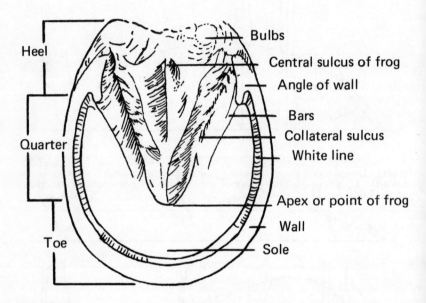

Heel

Quarter

Toe

Bulbs

Central sulcus of frog

Angle of wall

Bars

Collateral sulcus

White line

Apex or point of frog

Wall

Sole

Normal forefoot showing structures

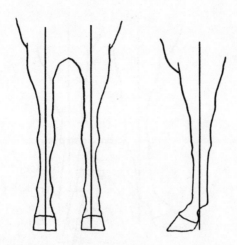

Good conformation

(LEFT)   Line dropped from the point of the shoulder joint bisects the limb
(RIGHT)   Line from the tuberspinae of the scapula bisects the limb as far back as the fetlock and drops at the heel

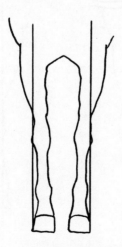

Poor conformation

Base narrow

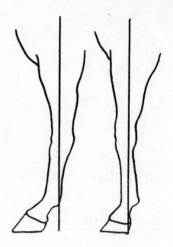

Poor conformation
(LEFT)   Calf knees—a posterior deviation of the carpus
(RIGHT)   Bucked knees—an anterior deviation of the carpus

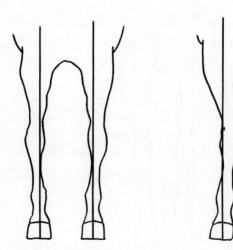

Poor conformation
Bow legs   Knock knees

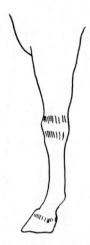

Poor conformation

Open knees

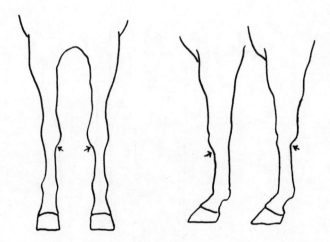

Poor conformation

Bench knees
(LEFT)   Tied-in knees, as indicated by the arrow
(RIGHT)   Cut out under the knees, as indicated by the arrow

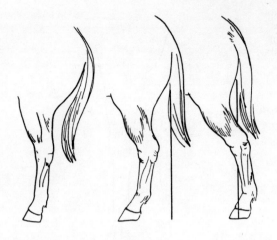

Poor conformation

(LEFT)   Too straight Behind
(MIDDLE)   Standing under Behind
(RIGHT)   Camped Behind

Poor conformation

Base narrow Behind

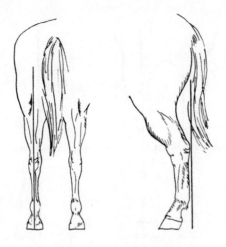

Good conformation

(LEFT)   Normal hind limbs
(RIGHT)   Normal hind limbs from side view

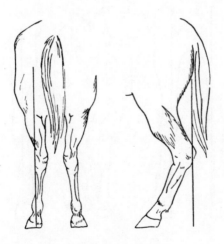

Poor conformation

(LEFT)   Cow hocks accompanied by base-wide conformation
(RIGHT)   Sickle hocks

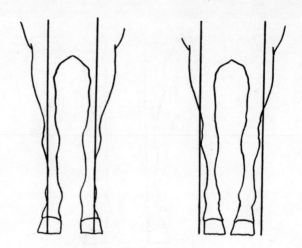

Conformation faults and effects

(LEFT) Base narrow, toe-out conformation
(RIGHT) Base narrow, toe-in conformation

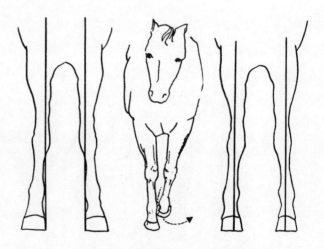

(LEFT) Base-wide conformation—distance between centre lines of the feet is wider than centre lines of the limbs at the chest
(MIDDLE) Winging is caused by a toe-out position of the feet
(RIGHT) Base-wide toe-in positioning of the feet

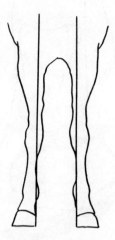

Conformation faults and effects
Base-wide toe-out positioning of the feet

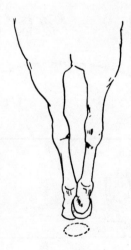

Plaiting

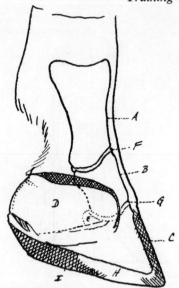

Section through normal foot showing correct angulation and parts of the foot

(A) 1st phalanx
(B) 2nd phalanx
(C) 3rd phalanx
(D) Cartilage
(E) Distil sesamoid
(F) Pastern joint
(G) Coffin joint
(H) Edge of wall of hoof
(I) Laminar corium

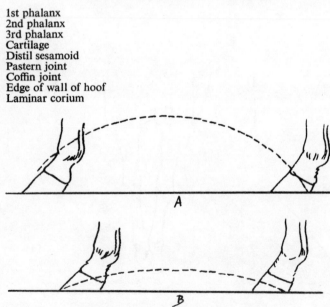

Conformation and its effect on action

(A) Normal arc of foot flight
(B) Low foot flight caused by lack of flexion in either the fore or hind limbs

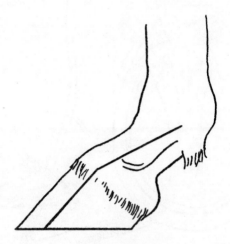

Poor conformation of the foot
Coon-footed. The foot axis is steeper than the pastern axis

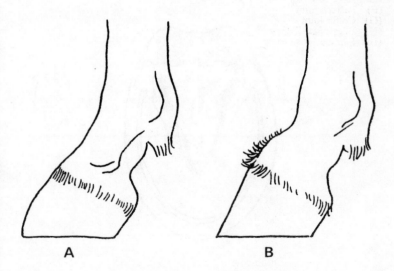

A

B

Bull-nosed foot

Buttress-foot

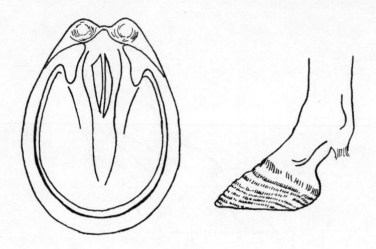

Poor conformation of the foot

(LEFT)   Contracted foot. Note narrowing of the heels and quarters
(RIGHT)   Rings in the hoof wall produced by chronic laminitis

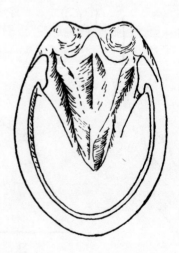

Good conformation of the foot

Normal hindfoot

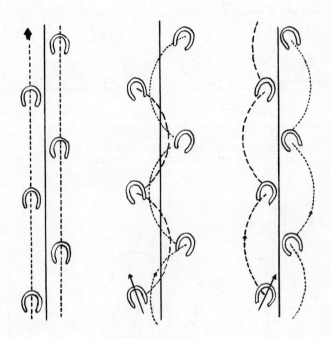

Conformation and action

(LEFT)   Normal footpath
(MIDDLE)   Footpath of a horse with toe-out conformation
(RIGHT)   Footpath of a horse with toe-in conformation

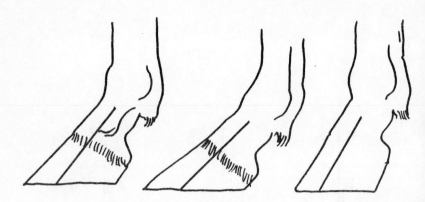

(LEFT)   Normal foot and pastern axis. Approximately 47 degrees.
(MIDDLE)   Foot and pastern axis less than normal
(RIGHT)   Foot and pastern axis greater than normal

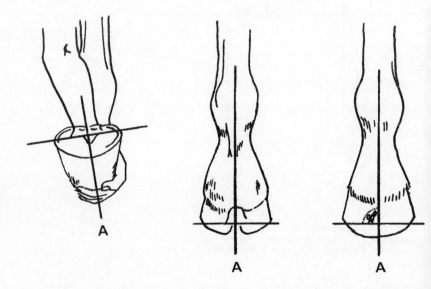

Line A shows foot and pastern axis as viewed from front and from behind.
This line should be straight with no deviation of the limb from the fetlock down.
The line crossing the foot axis at the ground surface is a line indicating foot level.
If the foot is level, these two lines form a 90 degree angle.

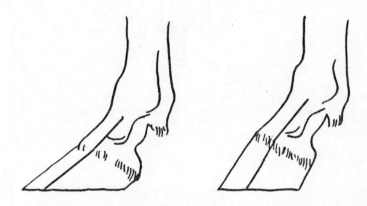

Poor conformation

(LEFT) Broken foot axis with toe too long and heel too low

(RIGHT) Broken foot axis with toe too short and heel too high

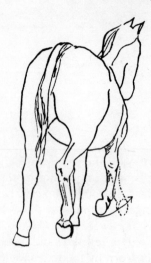

Paddling

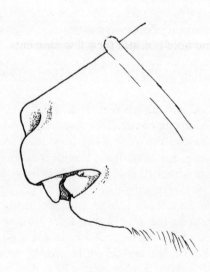

Carrot mouth

2 Pre-school

Handling the foal

Training really starts with the newborn foal. The sooner handling starts, the better. It is most important for the foal to learn to trust you and have confidence in you. If you can spend time quietly talking to the new foal and gently rubbing his neck and withers with your hands you will be making a very good beginning.

When the foal is only a few days old, introduce him to the 'foal slip'. This first halter worn by the foal should be made of very soft leather and be readily adjustable. You will find it quite easy to slip over the foal's ears and to fasten if you have already accustomed him to your voice and the touch of your hand on his neck, withers and head. Do not leave the foal slip on all the time as there is a danger of the foal catching his foot in it when scratching his ears, or becoming hooked up to a fence or gate.

Every day spend a few minutes with the foal. Perhaps in the loose box early in the morning before turning him out with his dam. Put the foal slip on and hold him still for a few moments. Then lead him a step or two towards his dam. If possible, have someone to help you by holding him while you gently run your hand over his body and down his legs.

After a few days, pick up his feet, very quietly, one by one. The foal will not yet be strong enough to resist and if you place yourself beside his shoulder and run your hand down the back of his front leg, at the same time gently nudging him over with your hips, you will find he learns this important lesson easily and quickly.

When the foal is thoroughly accustomed to your hands rubbing him gently all over, introduce him to a brush. Brush very gently at this stage, but removing the mud or dust from his coat will accustom him to the idea of grooming and also establish a good association of ideas—grooming is pleasurable—in his young mind. As soon as the foal understands about having his feet picked up and standing on three legs for a few moments, you may start picking out the mud with a hoof pick. Work carefully as the horn of a foal's foot is very soft, but if you work from heel to toe you will run no risk of digging the hoof pick into the sensitive parts of the foot, and you will assist the hoof to develop properly with a well developed frog and plenty of expansion in the heels.

First encounter with the blacksmith

When the foal is about three months old you can touch up his hooves gently with the rasp—or have your horse-shoer do it. Be sure you are present yourself and hold the foal. He should not resist or show any fear if you have done the preliminary work well, but if he does try to back away, hold him with an arm around his chest and another around his hindquarters. He will not then be able to move, and will gain courage from being held securely by someone he knows. It is a mistake to try to hold a frightened or resistant foal by the end of a lead shank only. He will twist and turn and probably rear and fight, and could easily end up hurting himself, as well as frightening himself. This sort of fright when the foal is young takes a great deal of time and patience to overcome and is unnecessary and avoidable.

Teaching him to lead and Catching up

The foal should be taught to lead beside his dam. Lead him very close to her at first and only gradually increase the distance between them as he gains confidence and understands that he has to obey you. If possible, have someone else lead the mare out from her loose box to her pasture each day, and you follow, leading the foal. Lead him equally from the right and the left side. Teach him to turn, following the mare, by pushing him gently away from you. Do not pull him round towards you, whether you are leading from the right or left.

During his first six months the foal should learn to be led on large circles, round corners, through gateways and both towards and away from his dam. It is very important that you lead him equally from the left side and the right side, since if you always lead and turn him to the same side, you are well on the way to developing a stiff, one-sided horse who only likes to turn one way.

Now is the time to form the habit of being easy to catch. If the mare comes when called and is easy to catch in the field, the foal will soon do the same. If he has not learnt this important lesson with his mother, then it must be one of the first things you teach him after he has been weaned. If you always reward him when he comes to you he will quickly gain confidence in his trainer and associate coming when called with some appropriate reward. Throughout his training, you must insist on obedience and discipline, and enforce them through reward and correction.

Trailering

Probably the foal will have to learn quite early in life about horse boxes or trailers. If the mare is to be bred again the foal may have to be boxed at seven or eight days old. Even if the mare does not visit the stallion, you may wish to enter your mare and foal in some shows, which is excellent training for the foal and introduces him to many new sights and sounds.

If you are travelling a mare and foal it is preferable to do so in a horse box, if possible, as there is more room inside and less chance of the foal being frightened, or squeezed or stepped on. If you have to use a trailer, take out the partition. The foal should not be tied up in the trailer, but may be held by someone travelling in the groom's compartment, or, if you have no one to help you, leave the foal loose, but tie the mare.

Either drive the trailer yourself or have someone driving who really knows how to handle the vehicle. It is an art to drive a car and trailer properly and far too few people take the trouble to learn how to go smoothly forward from a standstill, and drive slowly enough to avoid throwing the horses around. Stopping too sharply with a young foal in the trailer can cause serious injury as well as giving the foal a scare he may always associate with trailers.

Showing your mare and foal is excellent training for the foal. He will become accustomed to the noise and excitement of a show-ground, and it will give you a good opportunity to introduce him to motors, tractors and other animals, all with the calming influence of his mother close by to help you. This early training is of tremendous value later on, since horses have excellent memories and, if introduced properly to showing and handled quietly and calmly, they will form lasting "good associations". By the same token, roughness, over-excitement, bad experiences travelling, or other frights must be avoided.

Weaning

The foal who has been properly and kindly handled since birth will present much less problem at weaning time. If possible, wean two foals together so they have company during those first terrifying and lonely hours. If you cannot get another foal to be a companion for yours, try a pony or a donkey, or a goat, or even a chicken. It may sound unlikely, but a chicken can be an excellent companion for a lonely weanling.

The first winter

Not too much training can be done during the foal's first winter. Continue to handle, brush and lead him. Pick out his feet daily and have them trimmed regularly. You may introduce him to a rug and surcingle at this time, but he probably will not need it and if he is in at night and has grown a good thick coat, there is certainly no necessity to rug him up, unless you live in a very extreme climate. You may teach the foal to tie up at this stage, but NEVER leave him tied when you are not standing right there beside him. During the first two years of their lives, young horses have a terrible tendency to kill themselves by breaking their necks. Do not leave him tied, even if there is another horse close by and you just want to dash into the house for a second. That may be the fatal second, and it simply is not worth the risk.

The yearling

Training proper will probably recommence in the spring when your foal is a yearling. All his earlier training will now be confirmed by constant repetition. Groom him, pick up his feet, lead him about by himself. If you are lucky enough to live on a farm, lead him around the farm, on country roads where there is not too much traffic, and all round the village. Then take him along to intersections where there is a wide verge so that you can introduce him to some heavy traffic in safety and without having to get so close to it that he is frightened. Introduce him to dogs, cattle, pigs and sheep. Teach him to stand up square, with his weight on all four feet and to remain still until told to move off. Teach him to lead well at walk and trot—place yourself at his shoulder and look ahead. Do not look at the horse. Leave four inches or so between your hand and the head-collar and hold a whip in your outside hand (left if you are on the horse's near side, right if you are on his right). Walk forward actively and when you want to trot, use your voice to say "trot", click your tongue, and trot forward yourself. If he does not come along beside you, touch him with the whip on his flank. He will not even see the whip and should certainly not be made afraid of it, but a single gentle tap will probably be all that is necessary to help him to know what you want. Again, each time you halt make sure he stands up square with weight on all four feet and remains still until told to move. You should be able to move round him, stroke him, pat his rump, and so on, and he should remain still and attentive. Remember to reward and encourage him immediately he does what you ask. Your voice and a pat make excellent rewards but there is no harm in the occasional carrot. Do not make a practice of giving titbits after every correct response, however, or you will find your yearling becoming a nibbler, and maybe, later, even a biter.

A young horse, like a young child, investigates everything with his mouth. This is perfectly natural at this age, but must be gently discouraged as time goes on. Much saddlery can be ruined by being chewed up by an undisciplined yearling if it is left within his reach and he has nothing better to do. Rugs and bandages are also favourite things to chew.

Stable manners

Now is the time for your youngster to be confirmed in good stable manners. I know it is easier to remove him from the loose box before you muck out, but then he will not learn to stand still on one side of his box while you clean the other, nor to move over, and to get back from the door, on command. Start by picking up the droppings while he is in the loose box, and just shaking out the bed for the night. Teach him to 'get over' by telling him to do so in a quiet, firm voice and at the same time pushing him over with a light pressure of your hand. Where you place yourself in relation to the young horse has a tremendous influence on his reaction to any command. Remember that if you place yourself in front of him, or just diagonally in front of him, he will tend to move back away from you and/or turn his head away from you and consequently his hind end towards you. If you stand diagonally behind his eye on one side, your presence will tend to drive him forwards and his quarters will move away from you as he brings his head round towards you.

Think ahead, see exactly where you want to move him to, then place yourself in such a position that he is almost compelled to obey you. Give your commands quietly but with authority and nine times out of ten the horse will move over with no fuss. If he does not, then you are in the best possible position to insist on obedience, and you may only need to reinforce your voice with a gentle pressure of your hand to get the required result. A horse who is pleasant and easy to handle in his box is a joy to work around, and also has started to form the habits of good discipline which you will want to develop in every sphere of his future activities.

Showing at halter

Showing your yearling at halter can be a very enjoyable and rewarding summer occupation for you as well as being a most useful learning experience for him. If you can take him to shows you will confirm the good habits he started to learn as a foal. Being groomed, boxed and led about regularly are in themselves excellent training, and by going to a few shows you will also widen the experience of your yearling and accustom him to remaining calm and obedient in strange and exciting surroundings.

It is important to remember in training the yearling as in training the foal, that his attention span is short and lessons should be kept very short too. Three ten minute lessons a day are much better than one half hour lesson. During your lessons, teach the youngster to obey your voice, both outside the stable and inside. It will help in his later training if he already knows 'walk', 'trot', 'halt', 'stand', and so on, and be sure to lead and turn equally to the right and left hand to avoid one-sidedness developing later on.

Lungeing

I know people who teach yearlings to lunge, but I prefer NOT to teach the young horse to lunge until he is at least two. Lungeing puts quite a strain on the young bones and tendons just because the horse is required to go on a fairly small circle, and even though you might not intend to do more than walk him round you on the circle, if something startles him and he leaps around there is always the risk of injury or strain. So be patient, handle and groom your youngster, lead him about, by all means teach him to lead from another horse for a few minutes at a time if you have a suitable, calm, well trained 'schoolmaster' available which you may ride, but wait until he's more developed before starting seriously on the 'three L's', Loose schooling, Lungeing and Long Reining.

3 *The Three L's: [a] Loose Schooling*

The three-year-old

When training a horse it is important to remind yourself frequently that you have plenty of time. The trainer's worst enemy is likely to be haste. Basic training omitted when the horse is three years old can never be made up later, and if you have a promising young horse to train and you hurry things along at this stage, you will regret it later on.

Three years old is plenty of time to start a young horse's serious training. If he has been well handled all his life there will be no question of 'breaking him in', which I think is a most misleading term conjuring up all kinds of archaic horrors. If you have to deal with a horse which has not previously been handled at all, or, more likely, which has been mishandled, then the first thing you have to do is to overcome his fear and teach him all those vital lessons contained in the previous chapter.

I know that many people these days will start a young horse on his serious training at two years old. Personally, I do not like to do this. The horse, at two, is so very immature that he tires quickly, and his attention span is only a few minutes. Even if the trainer takes exceptional care, the young joints and tendons are very easily strained and permanent damage may result. I do not think it is worth the risk and I leave my young horses to grow until they are at least three and often four years old before starting serious training.

Loose schooling

Even before teaching the young horse to lunge, I like to loose school him. Loose schooling teaches the horse to respond to the voice commands, without subjecting his young joints to the sharp stops or changes of direction which may sometimes inadvertently occur on the lunge line. Some people leave out loose schooling altogether, either because they do not understand how to go about it, or because

they do not appreciate its value. Once you understand that the principle of loose schooling is exactly the same as the principle of
lungeing, that is, you are 'driving' the horse in front of you to make
him go forward, and placing yourself in front of him to make him
stop, then you are unlikely to have any problems.

The first lesson

Lead your young horse into the school (preferably an indoor school,
and not too large) with his headcollar and lead rope, and arm yourself with a pocketful of carrots and the lunge whip. It is important
that the horse should respect both you and the lunge whip, but he
must never learn to fear either. The whip is used to assist you in
keeping the horse moving forward at the required distance from
you, and it is worth while spending a little time learning how to use
the whip correctly.

When leading a horse from the near side, you should hold the
lead rope four inches or so from the horse's head with your right
hand; the end of the lead rope is in your left hand (never wound
round it), and the whip is also in your left hand, with the tip of the
whip held lower than the butt or handle, and always pointing behind
you. The lash is stretched along the length of the handle of the whip,
and is also held in your left hand—not allowed to trail along behind
you. If you are leading the horse from the off side, simply reverse the
above instructions. In teaching a horse to lead, it may be necessary
to raise the point of the whip slightly and touch the horse on his
hind leg, just below the hock, to encourage him to step forward
actively beside you.

Never carry the lunge whip like a fishing rod, never wave it about
aimlessly and never crack the whip, but learn how to flick the lash
accurately in the direction of the horse's hind leg by a small, controlled, movement of your hand and wrist.

Your first training session will, of course, be very short. Detach
the lead rope from the headcollar and encourage the horse to walk
forward to the track. In fact, to loose school a horse the trainer
simply 'walks the diagonals' keeping slightly behind the horse's eye,
and moving a fraction more behind the horse to quicken the pace,
and a fraction more in front of him to slow him down. But at first
the horse will not understand what you want from him and you will
have to make your commands very simple and obvious. Some young
horses will trot gaily away from you, some will plunge off and rush

about, and some will simply stand still beside you, not quite knowing what to do. Most horses, if pushed gently into the track, will trot on round the school, provided you keep yourself just behind their eye and walk actively towards their hindquarters. Depending on the size of the school, you will take five or six steps on the diagonal in one direction before turning and retracing your steps on the same diagonal in the opposite direction, always being careful to keep the horse in front of you. It is quite easy to do this in a small school, but if the arena is very large you will need an assistant to help you to keep the horse out on the track.

Voice commands

Decide on exactly what voice commands you intend to use through-out the horse's training and use them now. I find it easiest to get the horse going in trot first and then teach him to walk, and later on to canter. If he is trotting actively forwards he won't be so likely to take his attention off you and what you want from him. If you have to start the horse off by leading him into the track, be very careful not to get ahead of him.

Once he is moving forward, leave go of his headcollar and say, with an upward inflection 'Walk on' (or, if he is already trotting, say 'Trot'). Your object is to associate in the horse's mind the correct responses to your voice commands. Since, at this stage, you will not be able to make the horse do exactly what you say, you must say exactly what the horse does! This way, he will quickly learn to asso-ciate your voice commands with his own actions.

Do not use too many different words and do not 'chat' to the horse. Always use exactly the same word and the same inflection and tone of voice, and you will be surprised how quickly the horse learns what you want from him.

Send the horse round the school at trot a few times and then gradually slow him down by placing yourself a little in front of him saying at the same time, with a calm, downward inflection 'Waaa-alk, waaa-alk'. If he walks and you can send him on along the track in walk for a bit, good, but if he turns to come to you right away, encourage him to do so by saying "come boy" or simply 'come', holding out a carrot towards him, and stepping BACK, away from him, very slowly. It is important that the horse should come to you, not you go to the horse, unless he is one of the very placid variety who simply stands still and looks at you. If this is the case, go up to

him, take the headcollar, and then back away from him saying
"come, come" encouraging him to follow you.

Preparation for lungeing

The very first time you try to loose school your young horse, the
results may not be exactly what you had hoped for, but you will be
surprised how quickly both of you learn how to go about it. The
horse will learn the voice commands and he will also learn how to
manoeuvre himself in the confines of the indoor school. Properly
done, loose schooling is an excellent preparation for lungeing and
long-reining, and in the horse's later education it may be used in
teaching him how to jump. Keep your sessions very short—ten
minutes in the school is plenty. If you can take your horse into the
school for three ten minute sessions a day you will certainly be able
to teach him to 'walk', 'trot', 'canter', 'halt', 'stand', and 'come' in
a week.

The rest of his training at this stage will consist of repetition of
the work described in the previous chapter, together with his now
more thorough grooming sessions, and hopefully at least one hour a
day when he is turned out in the paddock to run free, and play, or
graze as he wishes.

Beware of 'programming'

One word of warning—every horse learns by repetition and it is his
superb memory which makes him so trainable. Be very careful indeed
to vary the order of your commands. You may always want to start
off with 'walk' but do not for ever more follow it with 'trot'. Sometimes walk the horse both ways round the school and halt him and
have him come to you before you trot, or trot him both ways round
before you ask him to walk. Sometimes trot him to the left first and
sometimes to the right—do not always start by trotting in the same
direction. Sometimes require him to stop and stand in the track, or
walk once round the ring before changing direction, sometimes call
him to you, sometimes reverse him in the track. Use your head and
consider the consequences of everything you do before you do it.
Above all, never be in a hurry.

4 *The Three L's: [b] Lungeing*

The start of formal education

Lungeing is an ideal way to start the formal education of the young horse, as well as being invaluable in retraining a spoilt horse who has lost his natural suppleness and become cramped in his movement. It will give your three-year-old his first experience of the driving and restraining controls of the rider, and will help to develop him physically and mentally, without putting the added strain of carrying a rider's weight on his young joints and tendons. By means of lungeing you can also provide your young horse with sufficient exercise to keep him healthy, teach him to reach forward for the bit and develop the long, balanced strides you want to encourage him to use later, when ridden.

The tack

During the time you are teaching your youngster to loose school, you can also accustom him to the equipment you will use to lunge him. He will, of course, already know and respect the lunge whip, since he will see you with it during the loose schooling sessions. You can introduce him to the lungeing cavesson, the surcingle or roller, and soft, protective bandages, by putting them on him quietly for a few minutes every day in his loose box. Be careful to tighten up the roller very gently if the horse is not used to wearing one, or you may create in him the objectionable habit of "blowing himself up" when being saddled.

The equipment used in lungeing includes the cavesson, which must fit your horse comfortably. It must have a very well padded nose-band which fits snugly over the bony bridge of the horse's nose. If it is too loose, or fitted too low, on the grisley portion of his nose, you will cause your horse unintentional pain. The cavesson is fitted with a jowl strap, which is designed to hold the cheek pieces back from the horse's eyes, and to give a snug fit. This strap should be sewn to the cheek straps at the same height as the outer corner of the horse's eye. Lungeing cavessons are fitted with a heavy, metal noseband, with a ring on either side and one in the centre front. These rings should be flat to the noseband and not attached to projecting lugs.

The surcingle or lungeing roller is used at first in place of a saddle. Later on you may wish to lunge in a saddle with the surcingle fitted over it, to allow the side reins to be attached to the surcingle rather than to the saddle. I prefer not to use side reins at all with a young horse, although they can be most useful in retraining a spoilt horse, or when training young stallions who, without them, will often be more interested in waving their heads in the air or snaking them along the ground, than in their lesson.

Since you are lungeing your youngster to encourage him to reach forward with his head, develop long, roomy, balanced strides, and encourage unconstrained movement, side reins seem to be, at this early stage, a contradiction. However, fitting the young horse with a surcingle prepares him for the saddle, which will come next.

Leg protection

Do not lunge a young horse without protective boots or bandages, and preferably teach him to lunge before he is shod. It is so easy for a three- or four-year-old, who has not yet gained full control of his limbs, to knock his legs and cause permanent lumps or scars, that it is well worth the little extra trouble to bandage him before work.

The lunge rein

The lunge rein itself is twenty-five to thirty feet long, made of soft hemp but preferably not too smooth and slippery, for although it must run through you hand easily, you do want to be able to hold onto it comfortably. The lunge rein may be fitted with a metal snap or a buckle fastening, but whatever the method of fastening, it must be mounted on a swivel, to avoid the lunge line from twisting when in use.

Last but not least, ALWAYS wear gloves yourself for lungeing or long reining.

The first lesson

It is certainly not impossible to teach your horse to lunge all by yourself, but it is very much easier if you can persuade a friend to help you with the first two or three lessons. If at all possible, start

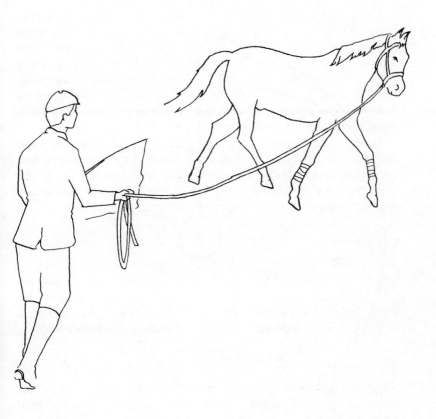

teaching your horse in an indoor arena. It will be much easier to
control him, and his attention will remain on you. If you do not have
an indoor school at your disposal, use the corner of a quiet field,
where you will have at least two fences to provide two sides of your
circle. If you have to lunge outside, on grass, you may be obliged
to use side reins, fitted loose enough for the horse to stretch his neck
but not long enough for him to reach the grass. If you do use side
reins, make sure they are both adjusted to the same length, and do
not attach them to the bit until immediately before you start
lungeing.

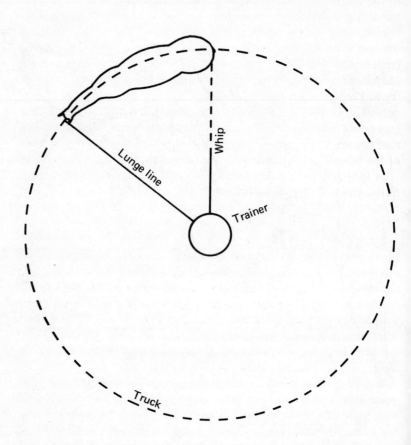

Keep it short

The first lunge lesson will, of course, be very short. Do not expect
everything to go completely smoothly the first time you try and do not
continue the lesson until the horse is tired, but stop after ten minutes
or so, as soon as you get a reasonably correct response.

Bring the horse into the school wearing his bandages, surcingle and cavesson, with the lunge rein attached to the cavesson. The ring in the centre front is designed for the attachment of the lunge rein, but this position of the rein does not suit all horses. Some young horses, with very sensitive noses, go forward much more freely if the rein is attached to the back of the noseband, or, if they have a tendency to pull away from you, to the side ring. Use your own judgement over this question of where to attache the lunge rein and try to keep an open mind. Much will depend on the type and temperament of the horse you are training, and your own skill and experience lungeing. If you decide to use the front ring, remember that you are applying a very magnified aid on a very sensitive portion of the horse and be particularly gentle in handling the rein.

In lungeing, as in every other phase of the training of the young horse, you will work equally to the right and the left. Let us assume, however, that you are going to start on the left rein, that is, your horse is going to describe a circle around you, travelling anti-clockwise.

Place your assistant, if you have one, on the right side of the horse. He will lead the horse by holding onto the cheek strap or noseband on the outside. Place yourself level with the left shoulder, the lunge rein carefully folded and laid loop on loop across your left palm, the whip, which must be long enough to reach the horse when he is travelling round you on a large circle (about twelve to sixteen feet overall), in your right hand, point held low to the ground, beside the near hind leg. At first you are going to walk round the whole rectangle of the indoor school and will not be lungeing at all, really. After the loose schooling sessions the horse will understand your voice aids, which will be a great help to you now. Say "Walk on" with your customary upward inflection and your assistant will lead the horse forward. You will also lead him forward with the lunge rein held only about three or four feet from his head in your left hand. Keep your right shoulder in advance of your left, so that you are facing the same direction as the horse, and, in fact, you drive him forward in front of you.

Make one or two complete circuits of the indoor school and gradually your rectangle will become an oval and your oval a circle at one end. Very gradually, pay out the lunge line and approach the centre of your circle. Once there, try to keep pretty much to one spot. It is easy, when lungeing, to confuse the horse by walking about too much. You should be turning around on one spot, not wandering all over the arena.

The hand

It is just as important to maintain a steady hand when lungeing as it is when riding. Try to maintain a steady, light contact with your horse through a slightly sagging line.

When your young horse has walked a few times round the circle and knows where he is supposed to go, provided he is quiet and relaxed, you may go on into trot. Say 'Terrot' and your assistant leads the horse forward into trot, and, still trotting along beside him, on the outside of the circle, quietly lets go of his cheek strap, leaving the horse free. Provided the horse continues to trot, the assistant can drop back to your right side, approximately half way between you and the horse. Now you will be leading the horse forward with your left hand and driving him forward with the whip, which is held in the right hand, pointing towards the horse's quarters, forming a V.

Free forward movement

In lungeing, as in loose schooling, it is important for the trainer to anticipate the actions and reactions of the horse.

Particularly in this very early stage of training, all you are trying to achieve on the lunge is free forward movement, and the same balance and regularity of stride as is natural to your horse at liberty.

Do not try to teach the horse too much all at once. Think ahead, and after he has trotted round two or three times you will see that he is ready to drop back into a walk. Take advantage of this moment to 'ask' your horse to walk. Saying 'Waa-a-alk' very soothingly and with a downward inflection of your voice, step sideways towards the perimeter of your circle (in this case, to your left) shortening your lunge line by looping it across your hand, and maintaining a light tension as you go. The horse, seeing you slightly ahead of him, no longer driving him forward, will slow down and walk, and you can then ask him to halt. Do not allow him to turn either into the circle or out from it, but ask him to stand still, on the perimeter. You then approach him and pat him and reward him with your voice, and perhaps a carrot.

Work equally to both directions

After a few circles on the left rein, reverse the horse by walking him round on a small semi-circle towards the centre of the lunge circle, and repeat the whole exercise to the right. Remember to work equally in both directions and to vary from day to day whether you start lungeing to the left or the right. Never let it become a confirmed habit to start off in one particular direction.

The whip

Some people like to start the horse's education on the lunge without carrying the whip, and the assistant, after he stops leading the horse, takes over the job of carrying the whip, pointing it towards the horse's hind legs, and positioning himself midway between the horse and the lungeing trainer. This is certainly a most useful method to adopt with a horse that is frightened of the whip, as it allows him to become accustomed to it and not to associate it directly with the trainer. However, since your young horse has been loose schooled before being lunged, he is already used to the whip and will not fear it. I prefer to carry the whip myself right from the start.

Balance and Bitting

Do not try to put your young horse into a canter on the lunge at this point, but work with him in walk and trot. A young horse, unaccustomed to work on the circle, may easily become unbalanced, slip, fall, or bang his legs, if asked to canter too soon on the lunge. If the horse has a very inactive trot, it may be a good idea to canter him fairly soon in order to encourage greater activity, and in this case the canter may actually improve his trot. But generally speaking you will spend most of the early lessons on the lunge in walk and trot.

After the horse is accustomed to working on the lunge, fit a snaffle bridle on him as well as the lungeing cavesson and allow him to get used to the feel of the bit. Be sure that the snaffle is correctly adjusted, since if it is too low in the horse's mouth he will start to play with it too much and in all probability will learn to bring his tongue over the bit. If it is very high, it will cause him discomfort and probably make him raise and shake his head, instead of lowering it and relaxing.

Impulsion

As soon as the horse is working well on the lunge, leave off the cavesson and attach the lunge rein direct to the snaffle ring on the inside of the circle. The lunge rein will then be giving a direct open-rein aid which the horse obeys by circling around the trainer. I find this an excellent method of introducing young horses to the action of the bit, but, of course, the trainer must be very light and quiet with his hands.

When the horse is beginning to develop his impulsion while retaining a uniform length of stride on the lunge, you may find it helpful to start using the side reins. Do not adjust them too short, they should leave plenty of room for the horse to lower his head and stretch his neck. But the more developed and balanced he becomes, the shorter you will adjust them, thus teaching the horse to come up to the bit and yield to it. Side reins can be useful, particularly in re-training a spoilt horse, but they also have drawbacks. A horse may learn to bend his neck too much and go over the bit, or hollow his back and raise his head and come above the bit, in side reins, so watch your horse closely for evasions if you decide to use them.

I prefer to train a totally green horse without side reins at first, and to move on fairly quickly from the lungeing stage to long-reining, in order to 'make the horse's mouth'.

5   *The Three L's [c] Long Reining*

Long-reining is definitely the best way of handling and developing the young horse before he is mounted, yet it is not universally practised as one would expect. In fact, many people shy away from long-reining, or even condemn it, without understanding how it should be done, nor the advantages it can bring the young horse.

Advantages of long-reining

Long-reining is an art. It takes skill, patience and hours of practice to learn to handle long reins properly. But it is an art very well worth developing for anyone who trains young horses. From the horse's point of view, there are many advantages to a course of long-reining before he is mounted. First of all, it develops tendons and muscles in a way that just lungeing can never do, without the horse being subjected to any weight on his back. Thus it prepares him to carry the rider's weight correctly and with ease later on.

Long-reining also teaches the young horse discipline. He is under far greater control than he can ever be on the lunge line. He learns the controls and the aids exactly as if he were being ridden. There are two reins, which are attached to the bit, so he learns the rider's rein aids, and the two reins also apply pressures to his sides, so he learns the rider's leg aids.

Mouthing

Your young horse will already have learned to respond to your voice. Now you have the control necessary to ensure his correct response every time. You can mouth the horse on long reins far more effectively than on the lunge using side reins because the long reins come directly from the horse's mouth to your hands and are not attached to some dead and unfeeling piece of equipment against which the young horse may very easily learn to pull, or lean with a dead mouth.

Long-reining has the added advantage of developing both sides of the horse's body equally, as the outside rein gives the trainer complete control of the hindquarters. You can teach the horse to use his hocks, and to canter on both leads. In fact, you can teach your horse nearly everything on the long reins that you can teach him mounted.

Equipment

The equipment you need for long-reining is much the same as the equipment for lungeing. It is essential to have some sort of enclosure to do it in. An indoor school is ideal, but failing that an outdoor enclosure with fencing high enough to prevent the horse trying to jump out of it, and free from any projections on which the reins might become caught or entangled. The footing should be good and if you have to work outside you should sprinkle the track of your arena freely with a mixture of sand and fine ashes or sand and sawdust or wood shavings. In fact, it is a good idea to cover the whole surface of the enclosure if you can, and not just the track. The important thing is not to try to work the horse on a slippery surface.

The tack you need is a plain snaffle bridle with a thick mouth-piece, preferably flexible rubber at first, and large rings, but without reins; and the roller you used for lungeing, with two large rings fitted about ten inches above the horse's elbows. Instead of the roller, you may prefer to use the saddle straight away. In this case you adjust the stirrup irons six to nine inches above the horse's elbows and secure them with a spare stirrup leather passed under the horse, on top of the girth. Later in the long-reining training, you lower the stirrups until they are only just above the level of the elbow.

You will also need your lungeing whip, and two webbing long reins, or lungeing reins, about one inch wide and twenty to twenty-four feet long, fitted with a good buckle on a swivel at one end, and either a loop or a knot at the other. This loop, or knot, is to prevent the reins slipping through your hand. Each rein must be quite separate, on no account try to long-rein the horse with reins that have been stitched together in the centre.

The first lesson on long reins

By the time your young horse has been through the two previous stages of loose schooling and lungeing he will have gained a great deal of confidence in you, his trainer, and he will also have learnt to respond to the voice aids, and to lunge quietly in both directions at walk and trot. The first few lessons on long-reins will teach him a great deal, but the very first time he has them fitted he may be scared by the feel of the rein round his quarters, so it is advisable to attach the reins to the rings of the bit and also the noseband, rather than attaching them directly to the rings of the bit only.

Some trainers pass the outside rein over the horse's neck, at the withers, instead of over his rump and round his hindquarters. This method is simply a step between lungeing and long-reining, so far as the young horse is concerned, and I prefer to go ahead straight away with the rein round the quarters since in this way the trainer has far more control over the horse if he tries to spin round or run backwards.

If it is the very first time in long-reins it is helpful to have someone to assist you. Attach the right rein to the ring on the side of the bit and noseband together, and gather it in your right hand, loop on loop, in the same way as an ordinary lunge line. Place your horse in the track, on the right rein, (clockwise) about the quarter marker, very near the corner leading into the short end of the school. Have your assistant attach the left rein on the left side in exactly the same manner as the right rein is attached, and pass the rein to you across the horse's neck. The assistant should then move completely out of the way, in case the horse jumps forward. Taking the left rein in your left hand, gently flick it down over the horse's tail until it rests just above the hocks, keeping your body positioned just to the right of the horse's right hind leg. At the same time, say "Walk on" and start to drive your horse forward in the track, walking with him round the school.

Unless he is extremely nervous, you are unlikely to have much reaction from your horse at all. He may kick at the rein behind him a couple of times, or he may tuck his tail down and scoot forwards a few steps. This is why you position him close to the end of the school, the very fact of having the end wall in front of him will slow him down and enable you to be in full control in a few strides. By the time you have made two or three circuits of the school the horse will probably be perfectly calm and already resigned to the rein above his hocks.

Now halt the horse by stepping slightly back, towards his quarters, and closing your fingers on both reins. Your assistant should approach him quietly and detach the outside, or left, rein and pass it through the stirrup iron on the left side of the horse and then attach it again to the left side bit ring and noseband. It is important to have the rein through the stirrup iron during normal work on long-reins to avoid it from slipping down and touching the horse below the hocks. This could upset him and it is always a criticism levelled at long-reining. If it does happen and you cannot reposition the rein quickly and safely, simply drop the rein and bring the horse to you with the inside rein. You will soon discover that even when things go slightly wrong, you have far more control over the horse long-reining than you had lungeing on one rein alone.

Work the horse on the long-reins in a large circle at walk and trot for about five minutes. You will find your downward transitions much easier and more accurate with the two reins. Then bring your horse to a halt and approach quietly, shortening the reins in your hands by holding both reins in one hand and sliding the other hand forward up the reins as you come. For the first few sessions have your assistant come to the horse's head and help you to reverse the position of the reins, later on you will have no difficulty doing this on your own. Pass the right rein through the right stirrup and then attach it to the bit and noseband. The left rein now comes directly from the horse's head to your left hand. You are now ready to work the horse on the left circle in walk and trot.

Manual dexterity

The whole art of long-reining consists in handling the reins and whip. Try taking both reins in the left hand when the horse goes left and keeping the whip in the right hand. Going right, reverse the positions of reins and whip. Sometimes you will want the reins one in each hand, and then you keep the whip in the outside hand as for lungeing, in addition to that rein.

Work on long-reins

As soon as your horse becomes used to the long reins, attach them directly to the bit rings. If you are still anxious about your handling of the reins and don't want all the feel to go to the horse's mouth, continue to attach them to the bit and the noseband.

Continue this stage, with the inside rein direct to your hand and the outside rein through the stirrup iron and round the quarters, for as long as possible. You are developing muscles, and tendons,

Major John Lynch long-reining *Happy Visitor*: a sequence of seven photographs (Chapter 5). *Photos Allen Studio*
1   The start of haunches-in

2   Rein back

3   Half pass right

4   Half pass right

5 Half pass left

6 Half pass left

7   Over a fence

The Englishman—a good type of thoroughbred with a good shoulder and plenty of bone. This horse is 17.1 hands (Chapter 1)

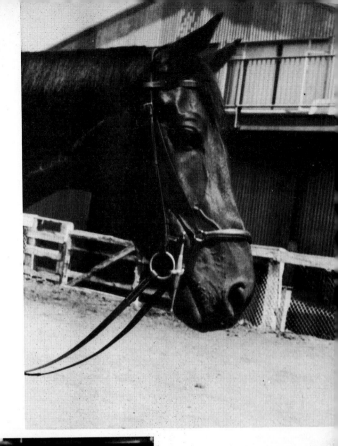

Correctly fitted snaffle with dropped noseband (Chapter 7)

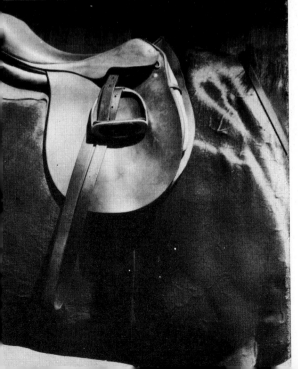

Correctly fitted saddle (Chapter 7)

The author on *Don Rossio*. The horse is yielding to the inside leg. His whole body is bent left as he performs a left circle in trot, but the hind feet follow the track of the forefeet. Note, no pulling on the left rein (Chapter 12). *Photo Nancy Bizzarro*

The author on *The Englishman*, trotting through cavaletti. The cavaletti are spaced at
4′ 6″ to 5′ depending on the stride of your horse. The rider should rise to the trot and
maintain very light rein contact with the bit. Note the activity of the horse and the bend in
the knee and hock (Chapter 14). *Photo Nancy Bizzarro*

The author on *The Englishman*, jumping with confidence. The fence is small—about 3′ 6″
with about 3′ spread—and therefore the horse has not 'folded' his front legs, but he is
jumping the centre of the fence, which has no wings and is not in the track, with calmness,
confidence and eagerness (Chapter 15). *Photo Nancy Bizzarro*

Over a fence—just leaving the ground (Chapter 15)

In the air (Chapter 15)

and educating the horse in mind and body. He is learning to obey, he is becoming more supple, and he is learning about the action of the bit. Keep the lessons short and rest the horse frequently. Long-reining is hard work for the horse.

The final stage of long-reining is when both reins are passed through the stirrup irons, or the rings on the roller and then to your hands. On no account move into this stage until the horse is really going forward freely and with rhythm. Now you will have complete control, but an inexperienced trainer could get into trouble with a green horse, so practise on a trained horse first.

Now you are in a position to do everything with the young horse that you can do mounted, but without the added strain of carrying a rider. You can work your horse on circles in both directions without stopping to change the reins over. You can teach the canter leads, the rein back, shoulder-in, half pass, serpentines, increases and decreases on the circle, and you can get your horse very fit.

Changing direction

To change direction on the circle, once you have both reins through the stirrup irons, is very simple. If the horse is going on a left circle, use the left rein and bring him towards the centre of the school, keep the reins in the left hand. When the horse approaches the centre, step forward with the right foot and run the right hand as far up the right rein as possible. Feel on the right rein and allow the left rein to slip through your fingers. The horse will now be on a right handed circle. Pass the whip from the right to the left hand behind your back.

Practise these changes at walk before trying them at trot or canter. Remember that it is important to keep up the pace and rhythm through the turn. Make certain that both you and the horse are very good at changes in trot before you try them in canter, but, provided the horse is ready for it, this is an excellent way to teach change of lead at canter.

Development of the horse

This work on long-reins develops the horse so much that by the time he has reached this stage he is physically ready to carry a rider.

You will probably be wondering how long this stage of your horse's training should last. If time allows, and the horse is young, three months at lungeing and long-reining would give the best results.

But in any case, you will want to spend at least six weeks at this stage of your horse's schooling. Far more progress can be made with the training on long-reins with an experienced trainer handling them than with an inexperienced but light rider on top of the green young horse.

Avoid boredom

The chief danger in this stage of your training will be boredom. Keep your sessions short. Reward the horse with carrots or apples. Vary his work by having him led out in hand for fifteen minutes or so both before and after long-reining, and sometimes, instead of long-reining, or in addition to it, ride a quiet, older horse, and lead your young horse alongside. You will have to choose your route carefully to avoid too much work on hard roads and of course you will want to avoid traffic, but this, too, can be a very useful part of the education of your young horse.

6 *Mounting for the First Time*

Preparation

When you have been lungeing and long-reining for about two months, your young horse will be ready to be mounted for the first time. Do not attempt this next step in his training until he is thoroughly accustomed to wearing a saddle and bridle, and to being lunged with the stirrups hanging loose, as well as being long-reined.

It is most useful to have an assistant to help you with this first mounting of your horse. Your assistant should be fairly light, and a confident rider who knows you and your methods well, so that there will be no breakdown of communications between you in the unlikely event of any emergency.

For several days before you intend to back your young horse, make a point of slapping the saddle with your hands on both sides of the horse, and pressing down on the stirrups with your hands, so that he becomes aware of the movements and noises made by a saddle, and a rider. Lead your horse to the mounting block and have your assistant stand on the block, so that the horse becomes accustomed to seeing someone above the normal level. It is surprising how many people forget that a young horse may become quite alarmed by seeing someone above his own eye level. Perform these exercises by the mounting block, from both sides of the horse, for several days, after his usual work on the lunge or long-reins for that day.

Actual mounting

When the horse quietly accepts these new positions of the trainer or assistant as normal, it is time to take the final step to mounting. Work the horse as usual, and at the end of the lungeing or long-reining session lead him to the mounting block, again as usual. This time, the assistant will place his hands on the saddle and very gently lie across the horse's back. Meanwhile, the trainer stands in front of the horse, slightly to one side, to prevent him from moving forward or back.

Getting on gradually

It is a good idea to put a stirrup leather round the horse's neck, as a 'holding-on' strap, so that your assistant has something other than the reins to grab if the horse should try to dislodge him. Most young horses, if they are properly prepared, take little or no notice of the person leaning over the saddle, but become engrossed with the oats or carrots the trainer offers them at the same moment.

The assistant should lean across the saddle from both sides and should also place a foot in the stirrup and put some weight in it, before attempting to complete the manoeuvre. Depending on the young horse, it may be wise to take two or three days over this intermediate stage, before going one step further and having your assistant slide his right leg across the saddle and sit gently down on the horse. In any case, once there the assistant must not fall off, whatever happens.

It is very unlikely indeed that the horse will try to dislodge the rider, but if he does 'put up a show' it is the assistant's job to stay put, on top of the horse, and the trainer's job to bring the horse to a halt as quickly as possible.

Your young horse probably will not object at all to a rider sitting on his back, so long as he is standing still. It is when he moves forwards, and becomes aware of the extra weight, that trouble, if there is to be any, is most likely to come. Remember that in his wild state the horse was liable to attack by wolves or mountain lions who might jump from a rock or tree onto his back, and attempt to hang on there and break the horse's neck. Instinct is still very strong in the horse and if he is allowed to become upset he reverts to instinctive actions and quickly forgets all his newly learned lessons. His instinctive reactions to something clinging to his back will be to buck and to run away. Your assistant should, therefore, refrain from using his legs at all and sit lightly on the horse, talking gently to him and stroking his neck. You, the trainer, can also help by holding the horse still and quiet, talking to him, giving him a carrot, and keeping the lunge rein sufficiently short so that he is always in complete control.

The first steps

When your horse allows the assistant to mount him and sit quietly on his back, it is time to take the first few steps forward with a rider on board. Lead the horse forwards whilst your assistant sits quietly in the saddle, holding the reins and the neck-strap, and otherwise doing nothing. Just take a few steps forward then halt and make much of the horse. Then take a few more steps, then another halt, and in a little while, make one or two turns. Within a few days you will be able to start to lunge the horse in walk with your assistant riding him. Again, just walk and halt, walk and halt. Keep the circle fairly small and the lunge rein short, even though this will mean that you must walk a fairly large circle yourself.

You may try a few steps in trot as soon as the horse is accustomed to the walk. Your assistant must be careful not to use his legs as yet. It will take a day or two for the horse to become accustomed to having a rider on his back and use of the legs will only frighten and confuse him at this stage. It is advisable to rise to the trot straight away, as sitting puts an extra strain on the young back. Keep the lunge rein fairly short and gently push the horse forward into trot for one or two circles. The rider should keep enough feel on the reins to prevent the horse from putting his head down between his knees and bucking, but the lighter the feel at present, the better.

If the horse arches his back and you think he is going to buck, urge him forward into a slightly stronger trot. This will divert his attention and he will probably forget all about bucking, which, in any case, is more difficult for him to do when moving actively forwards. If he does buck, try to get his head up as quickly as possible, without undue jerking on the lunge or reins.

Transitions and regular practice

After one or two circles in trot, the rider should sit down in the saddle and say 'waa-a-alk' at the same time as you ask the horse to come back to a walk. Walk for a little, then halt and reverse the horse and repeat the exercise in the opposite direction.

From this stage on it becomes a matter of increasing the time the rider spends in the saddle, and gradually teaching the young horse to respond to the aids of the rider rather than the person lungeing. Even a horse who is comparatively fit through lungeing and long-reining will tire surprisingly quickly when first asked to carry a rider, so the length of the mounted sessions must be increased only gradually. It is a good idea to dismount every ten minutes or so, at first. Not only does this rest the horse's back, but it also confirms his training in being mounted.

Be sure to mount from both sides equally, and not always from the near side. Insist that the horse stands quietly and allows you to take up the reins and place your foot in the stirrup iron without moving. If he tries to move forward when you mount, gently restrain him with the reins and your voice, remove your foot from the stirrup iron, and start all over again when the horse is standing still. If he tries to move backwards, stand a little further towards his tail, close to his body, facing his head, to mount. This proposition will have a slightly forward driving effect which is usually sufficient to prevent a young horse from stepping back.

When the rider is in the saddle do not allow the horse to move off immediately. Require him to stand still and quiet so that you can adjust stirrups, and later on, the girth, gather up the reins and only then ask him to move forwards. It will take a little more time and effort to teach these manners to your young horse, but you will reap the reward of this extra labour all the life of the horse.

Work off the lunge

When the horse stands quietly to be mounted, moves forward at walk and at trot in both directions on the lunge, and will come back

Riding on the lunge

from trot to walk and from walk to halt at the request of the rider, he is ready to be ridden off the lunge. This will usually be after about a week of riding him on the lunge. During this period the rider very gradually begins to use his legs and hands at the same time as the trainer gives the aids by voice and by lunge, whip or rein. The horse will have a very fair idea of what the rider means by the actions of his legs and hands due to his training on long reins, but it will take a few days for him to make the necessary adjustments and learn to obey these signals when they are given to him by someone on his back. It will take him even longer to learn to balance himself with the added weight of the rider in the confined space of an indoor school, or even an outdoor arena.

Work at canter

A word about the canter. All the work described in this chapter should be performed at walk and trot. The horse's regular work on the lunge or on long reins should continue during this time, also, and can include some work at canter, but the canter, mounted, has no place here in the first few weeks of mounted training. If your horse is going remarkably well and seems happy and balanced, it may be a great temptation to canter him—'just to try out his gait'. Do not give in to this temptation.

The young horse must develop a great deal of confidence, change his whole balance, and become much more certain of the meaning of the rider's aids before he can canter satisfactorily with a rider on his back, so you would not learn much about his gait even if you did canter him now, and you might easily frighten him, by letting him discover that he was not truly in control of his limbs, with the added weight of the rider and the tight corners to be negotiated. He might also, quite easily, start bucking, or at least bouncing, through sheer exhilaration of movement, and you might find yourself having to use far stronger rein aids than you would wish to bring him back under control. Much better to make haste slowly and stick to the walk and trot for some weeks, until you and your horse have developed well established lines of communication and good balance and confidence.

7 *Correct Bitting and Saddle Fitting*

Now that your young horse is quiet to mount and understands your aids enough to walk and trot around the indoor school, he is ready to move on into the second stage of his elementary mounted training. Provided he is strong and well developed, this stage may be started in the spring of his three year old year. It seems to be the fashion at present to train horses ever younger and younger, but although it may not be actually harmful to mount the youngster and take his training to the level described in the previous chapter, during the late fall of his two year old year, it certainly is harmful to proceed any further until he is at least three, and preferably four years old.

If you have mounted your youngster at two, you should let him grow and develop during the winter, and then repeat and confirm all previous training, particularly lungeing, long-reining and mounting, the following spring or summer, before progressing to the next stage.

Developing obedience

The objectives to be attained at this stage are, confidence, obedience and suppleness. Your young horse must learn to move freely forward, on the bit, although still in a long frame and with the head low and the neck long, and to be responsive to the rider's legs and hands. Keep these objectives in mind all the time you are working with him.

Bitting

Correct bitting is very important. All the elementary training of the young horse should be done on the snaffle, and there are many different types. A thick, jointed snaffle, with cheek pieces, but with a loose ring attachment, is probably the most satisfactory for most young horses. The cheeks on the bit prevent it from being pulled through his mouth, and they also prevent the bit from rubbing the sides of the horse's mouth. The leather keepers, which hold the cheeks of the bit to the cheek straps of the bridle, prevent the bit from turning over in the horse's mouth, and hold it still, so that it is always in the

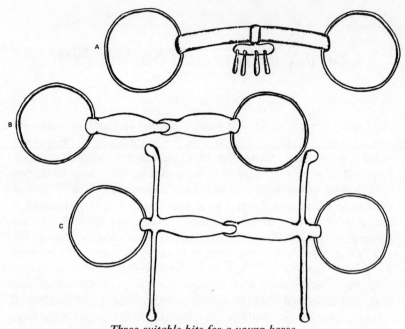

Three suitable bits for a young horse
(A) Key bit helps keep the mouth moist   (B) Thick, mild wire ring snaffle in rubber or metal   (C)   Full cheek snaffle—the Fulmer is the best design

same position. They also help to prevent the young horse from catching hold of the lower branch of the cheek of the bit with his lips and playing with it; but if your horse does develop this habit, it is better to stop using a cheek snaffle and use a ring snaffle instead. The loose ring on the bit (as opposed to the fixed ring on an eggbut snaffle, for example) enables the horse to move the bit a little, which encourages him to champ it slightly and is a great help with a young horse who tends to be dry in the mouth, or who opens his mouth on the slightest pressure of the bit. If the horse is too moist mouthed, it is better to use a cheek snaffle with a fixed, rather than a loose ring, attachment, or an eggbut ring snaffle.

Correct adjustment

If a jointed snaffle is used, take care to get a bit the correct width for your horse's mouth. If it is too narrow it will pinch the corners of the mouth, and if it is too wide, it will bruise him, and the joint may well drop down too low in the mouth and bang against the back

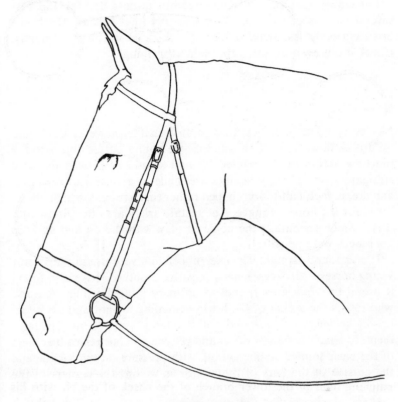

A well fitting snaffle

of the front teeth. This is not only uncomfortable for the horse, but is also an open invitation to him to put his tongue over the bit.

It is worthwhile taking time and trouble to ensure that the bit is not only the correct size for the horse, but also that it is correctly adjusted, so that it rests comfortably in the corners of his mouth, just folding his lips without pulling them up, and that it is held in position by the cheek straps and not simply by the horse holding it up in his mouth. You can check this by standing nearly in front of the horse and gently opening his mouth with your thumbs or fingers, one hand on each side of his mouth. Place the index finger of each hand on the bit and gently pull it down in the mouth. If it does move down, away from the corners of the lips, then the horse has been obligingly holding it in position for you and you should adjust the cheek straps accordingly.

Remember that new leather stretches quite a lot for the first several months of use, and do not assume that because the bridle fitted correctly last week or last month it must still fit correctly. Check it out every so often throughout training.

Other bits

Not every horse goes best in a jointed snaffle, however thick and mild it is, however well adjusted. Some young horses object to the pinching action of the jointed bit and should be started out in a straight snaffle. Straight snaffles are made in a variety of materials and are, in fact, half-moon shaped rather than straight, which allows room for the horse's tongue. The metal variety are often fitted with 'keys' which encourage the horse to play with the bit and so keep his mouth wet and soft.

I have found straight, flexible rubber bits very useful with some young horses with exceptionally sensitive mouths. I have also found it useful to wrap latex round an ordinary jointed snaffle. A horse who resists the action of the bit by stiffening his jaw and neck and raising his head, may respond well to a latex wrapped bit. The latex seems to have a softening effect and yet you still have the advantages of the basic jointed snaffle action, with pressure on the tongue and the outside of the bars of the mouth as well as the corners of the mouth.

If you are unhappy with the results you are getting from your horse in the bit you are using at present, then by all means try a change, but do come to a decision about which bit works best for you and your horse at the stage you are at, and then stick to it for a while. I have heard people say 'Oh, I have found the key to my horse's mouth, I change the bit every day and he never knows what to expect so he obeys it!' but I believe that with this philosophy you are more likely to confuse your horse than to train him and he may simply be learning to evade the action of the bit in more ways than you can discover how to control.

Whatever bit you decide to use, be sure that not only does it fit your horse correctly and is correctly adjusted, but also that it is in good sound condition. Never use nickel bits that are worn or rough, or rubber bits that have been chewed through. There is far too much danger of damaging your horse's mouth by using a bit that is in less than first class condition to make it worthwhile.

The bridle

The leatherwork of your bridle, also, should be kept in good shape. See that it is regularly cleaned and soaped and that the stitching is in good repair. This will make it easier for you to adjust the bit whenever necessary, and will also protect you from unnecessary accidents which might happen if your stitching or leatherwork broke at a crucial moment.

It is a good idea to use a noseband with all snaffle bridles. Some people advocate using a dropped noseband, fitted below the bit, right from the start. Certainly this will effectively prevent a horse from crossing his jaw or opening his mouth wide, but whether it 'teaches' the horse anything is debatable. Many young horses will fight a dropped noseband and I do not use it myself as a general practice, unless the horse shows a definite tendency to the above evasions. A cavesson noseband, fitted about two finger's breadth below the cheek bones and fastened so that there is room for two fingers between the noseband and the horse's nose, will have a similar effect on a young horse without the feeling of restriction associated with a dropped noseband.

If you do use a dropped noseband, it must be fitted very carefully. It must not be too tight and the upper strap must be fitted sufficiently high not to interfere with the nostrils and therefore the horse's breathing. The lower strap should rest comfortably in the chin groove.

If your horse is to progress happily in his training, it is important that he should be comfortable during your training sessions. All the trouble you take to see that he is correctly fitted in the right type of snaffle will pay off in the end since the horse will not be distracted from his lessons by a too tight brow-band pinching his ears, or a bit banging against the backs of his teeth.

The saddle

The fitting of the saddle is no less important, but is often rather more difficult, since a three year old is still growing and his withers have not formed properly. Take care to get a saddle that is not too wide for your horse, so that the pommel is pressing down on his withers, nor too narrow, so that the panels are pinching his shoulders and spine. Saddles generally come in three widths, narrow, medium and wide. Any good saddler will help you to fit your horse correctly.

Make a note of the horse's age, height and type; then measure his back, and take all the information to your saddler.

Measuring the back

To measure the horse's back, take a piece of flexible lead or electric cable, about eighteen inches long. Shape this over the horse's withers at a point approximately where the head of the saddle would lie, and press it well down to the shape of the back. Trace the outline of the shape obtained onto a piece of paper and mark the respective sides 'left' and 'right'. Take a second measurement in exactly the same way nine inches to the rear of the first. Take the final measurement along the length of the back from the withers. It is a good idea, also, to measure the girth of your horse, all round his body, close behind the withers.

All this information should enable you to get a saddle which fits your horse well. A saddle with a deep, central seat and a narrow waist and not too much stuffing—preferably no thigh roll, will be the best for your own correct position. To make quite sure the saddle does fit the horse, try it on with a rider sitting on it. You should have plenty of room at the pommel to place your hand between the saddle and the horse. You should be able to see a channel of light all along the horse's back. With the rider sitting on the saddle, pick up one of the horse's front legs and extend it forwards. There should be easy room for you to slide your hand between the horse's shoulder and the panel of the saddle. Look at the saddle from behind the horse. It should sit close to him (allowing for the free channel of air along the spine) with the weight of the saddle and the rider evenly distributed over the horse's back on that part where the ribs go straight out sideways from the spine. It is permissible for some of the weight to be carried on the ribs where they start to curve, but this should be only at the very top. Any undue pressure here will restrict the expansion of the horse's chest and so affect his breathing and therefore his ability to do the work expected of him.

Care of the back

Remember that the horse's back changes shape when he is at grass and when he is working, so it is best NOT to measure him for a saddle when he is fat.

Care of your horse's back extends beyond simply getting a saddle that fits correctly. Probably more sore backs are caused by riding a 'soft' horse for too long before his back has had a chance to harden, or failing to let his back cool before unsaddling after work, than any other reasons.

Finally, remember to saddle up carefully and gently, never slap the saddle down hard on to your horse, place it lightly on his back and slide it carefully into position. And then mount correctly, placing the left hand on the horse's neck and the right hand on the far side of the saddle, so that you will not pull the saddle out of position during mounting.

8   *Elementary Training—Free Forward Movement*

This stage of your horse's training is concerned with gaining his confidence, teaching him obedience, suppling his body and making him responsive to the rider's seat, leg and hand aids.

The aids

Right from the start your horse must learn to move freely forward in response to the rider's legs. At first, the leg aids will have to be used in conjunction with the voice and the whip. It will take the horse a little while to recover his natural balance under the weight of a rider. He must go straight, his head and neck must be allowed to find their own position, and the reins must be held long. Certainly no effort should be made to 'collect' him. At the walk there should be only the very slightest contact on the reins until the horse has learned to accept a contact on the bit at trot.

Transitions

If the horse is sent actively forward at trot and encouraged to take long, level strides, he will gradually accept a contact and eventually he will seek it, by stretching his neck and reaching for the bit himself. This will take time and you must work towards it by keeping your hands low and still, seeking only the lightest contact at first, making increases and decreases in pace, transitions from walk to trot, and trot to walk, to halt, to walk, to trot—and not always in the same order; all done very gradually, interspersed with frequent halts. The aid to halt is given primarily with the rider's seat—he ceases to follow the horse's movement with his back and seat and the horse stops.

Frequent transitions are really the key to this work. They teach the horse to find his balance with the added weight of a rider and they help him to develop the necessary muscles.

Work programme

At first you should work on straight lines, or around the outside track in the riding school or training arena. When trotting, change the diagonal frequently, and always when you change direction. If you fail to change the diagonal and always ride on the same diagonal, your horse will become very stiff and one-sided. Every period of trot must be followed by a period of walk, to rest the horse. This should sometimes be walk on a loose rein, when there is actually a slack loop of rein between the rider's hand and the bit, and sometimes walk on a long rein, when the rider allows the horse to stretch his head and neck but remains lightly in contact with his mouth. The actual duration of the periods of trot must depend on the strength and condition of the horse, but be very careful not to ask more from him than he is physically able to give, or you may discourage him and make him sour to his work.

Whenever you change direction in the school at this stage, do so in walk, across the diagonal. If you are working in an arena with other horses, be careful to choose a moment when you will not meet any other horse on the diagonal.

Understanding and obedience

The aids you use must be very clear and definite. They may even be a little exaggerated if necessary. Remember that with a young horse there is a much longer time lapse between the rider giving the aid and the horse interpreting it and obeying it than there is with an experienced, trained horse. You must certainly insist on obedience, but give the young horse plenty of time to understand the aid and to adjust his balance and carry it out.

Frequent halts are very useful. Always bring the horse to halt through walk, at this stage. Make him stand up squarely, with his weight evenly distributed on all four feet. The length of time you ask him to stand still will depend on his temperament, physical fitness, and stage of training.

The best time to teach the horse to do good halts is just before you finish your work for the day. Bring him to a square halt, and when he stands perfectly still for a few seconds, dismount. This way, the dismount becomes a reward for the good halt, and the length of the halt can gradually be increased.

Circles

When your horse is going well at walk and trot round the whole
arena in both directions, you can start working him on large circles.
Most young horses who have been properly prepared through
lungeing and long-reining have little difficulty with a large circle. If
you do experience difficulty making the horse understand what you
want, use an open rein to the inside. Some horses are very quick to
learn and some are very slow and become easily muddled, so it will
pay dividends to know your horse thoroughly, both in and out of the
stable. Remember that the horse goes where the rider looks, so turn
your head and look around your circle—the horse will follow your
eyes.

Lightness and co-ordination of the aids

Although your aids must always be quite clear and definite, you
should use the lightest possible aid to achieve the result you desire.
Ultimately, your aids should be invisible to an observer but still
remain clear to the horse, so do not start by using over strong aids.
Always place your horse in such a position that it is impossible for
him to give the wrong response, and then apply your aids. Absolute
harmony of your body, legs and hands is essential, and at first,
through corners and large circles you will use just the inside rein.
When the horse is moving freely forward and understands the aids,
it is important to use both reins and also your legs through corners
and circles. Using the inside rein only will turn the horse's head and
neck and his body will follow but it will also have the effect of
throwing the quarters out from the turn and the horse is thus avoiding
stepping deep under his body and using the joints of his hind legs.
When both reins are used in corners and turns, combined, of course,
with the use of the legs, the action of the inside rein will become
effective all through the horse's body and will supple the whole of
the horse, and especially his inside hind leg.

Keep lessons short

The back muscles of a young horse will tire very quickly at first, so
your mounted lessons will be very short to begin with, only about
ten to fifteen minutes. As the back becomes stronger increase the
length of time spent riding the young horse, but be careful to follow

every period of trot with a rest period at walk, and always end each lesson with a period of walk on a loose rein. You will want to reward your horse for a correct response, and rest is an excellent reward.

When you are teaching a new exercise, do not repeat it and repeat it until the horse becomes soured with it. Perform it once or twice, three times at most. Provided you are getting a reasonable response, stop the horse and rest. Don't expect the same quality and consistency of response from a young horse in his first few weeks of mounted training that you would expect from a trained horse.

Headcarriage

All the work in the first few months should be at walk and trot. It is very important at this stage to remember to allow the horse to carry his head as low as he wants and on no account should you try to pull his head up or to obtain collection. Concentrate on free forward movement, with long, swinging, rhythmic strides.

Keeping the horse interested

Probably the biggest problem you will encounter at this point is avoiding boredom and sourness for your young horse. As his back grows stronger and you are able to ride him for longer periods, there is always a temptation to ask too much of him or to repeat and repeat an exercise he is doing quite satisfactorily. Keep alert yourself and concentrate fully on what you are doing. A great deal of your work will consist of transitions, both up and down, between halt, walk, and trot. Be careful not to ask for halt, for instance, in the same place in the arena more than once or twice in a row. If you do, you will already have started a habit in the young horse to halt at a given spot, rather than to halt at a given aid.

I believe that it is a good idea to introduce a pole on the ground about now and to accustom your youngster to walking over it in both directions, and then to trotting over it. This not only adds variety and interest to his work, but also helps him to stretch his neck and use his back, and supple his knees and hocks and develop the muscles of his loins and shoulders. Provided the horse is progressing well and showing no signs of fear, or sourness, I would have no hesitation in increasing the single pole on the ground to three poles at four and a half feet distance over which I first ask the horse to walk, and then to trot.

Trotting poles

Trotting poles are an invaluable part of the training and physical development of every young horse. They should be spaced according to the size of the horse. They may be used to help to lengthen the stride, in due course, but at first they should be placed at an easy and natural distance for the young horse. If he is neither excessively large nor very small, four and a half feet will probably prove to be a comfortable distance. But poles may be set anywhere from four feet to six feet apart eventually. If you have cavaletti, use these rather than poles on the ground as they are safer. A cavaletti on its lowest height will not roll if the horse steps on it, which is what happens with poles lying on the ground. This can cause a horse to wrench a joint or muscle unnecessarily.

As you ride through the poles, or cavaletti, stay at rising trot and slightly accentuate the forward inclination of your body. Keep your hands very low and still and allow the horse as much rein as he wants to take, so that he may really lower his head, stretch his neck and use his back.

Hacking

This stage of training is also an excellent time to introduce your youngster to the outside world. If you have been able to long-rein him, or even lead him, along quiet side roads and introduce him to traffic during his early training, this 'hacking out' will not be so traumatic. But in any case, going out under saddle for the first time is likely to be quite an exciting experience for any young horse and it is a good idea to have someone with you, riding a quiet and experienced horse, who will act as a schoolmaster for the youngster.

At first, walk along side by side, if this is possible, or let the young horse follow the lead of the experienced horse. But soon become a little more demanding and ask the young horse to pass his companion and take the lead. Then you can allow the older horse to pass you, and you ask the young horse to stand still and quiet whilst the other horse passes and continues on his way. Next ask the young horse to catch up and pass the older horse. Even if this is only done in walk and trot, it can be very valuable training indeed, since this is the time to ensure that your horse will move happily and freely forward, away from his stable, away from his friends and companions, or towards them, without getting over-excited, and also that he will allow his friends to pass him, and yet remain quiet.

Shoeing

A word here about shoeing may be appropriate. I recommend leaving a young horse unshod as long as possible. If his feet are hard and healthy and kept regularly trimmed and he is working mainly in an indoor arena, he really does not need shoes, unless he is living in a particularly rocky pasture or is showing signs of being sore. The concussion caused by shoeing can do great harm to his young legs and should be avoided as long as reasonably possible.

Once you start hacking out, however, you may find it necessary to have your youngster fitted with his first set of shoes. These should be lightweight and very carefully fitted by a kind and experienced horseshoer who knows his job thoroughly. I often have front shoes only put on a young horse the first few times he is shod, since it is the front feet take most of the wear and tear and many horses manage quite well without hind shoes for several months.

A young horse introduced to shoeing with patience and common sense will never give you any trouble later on. You will have developed so much confidence in him that he will, by now, completely accept and trust human beings. Anyone who has owned a horse who has been wrongly handled when first being shod will appreciate what a blessing this confidence of the horse will be all through his life.

The basis of training

The work outlined above, performed regularly, with a tactful trainer who knows when to stop and rest, and when to ask a little more from the horse, not only lays an excellent training foundation for a pleasant, happy riding horse, but will also enhance the physical beauty and muscular strength of the horse. Correct training, coupled with good feeding and grooming, will develop in the horse the correct muscles and harden his tendons, and so begin to shape him into a more beautiful and more healthy horse. In fact, I would go so far as to say that if your horse does not become more beautiful to look at during his training, then it is an indication that something is not going right in his training.

9 *Loose Jumping and Lungeing over Fences*

Jumping, over very small obstacles, is a valuable part of the early training of every young horse, and at this stage of his training your horse is ready to start loose jumping.

Improving natural balance

Loose jumping will improve his natural balance and teach him to be athletic. It will also give him confidence and create in him the desire to move freely forward, and also to jump. Most horses thoroughly enjoy loose jumping and it is a useful means of keeping the horse from getting bored, and, at the same time, developing his muscles.

Before starting loose jumping, lead your horse over small obstacles, both inside the school, and out in the fields. Small logs, a pole in a gateway, small ditches, are all inviting little jumps. Your horse will very quickly gain sufficient confidence in you to follow wherever you lead, and if you are using trotting poles in your school work, they will already be having a strengthening effect on his muscles and back.

The jumping lane

The best way to loose jump is in an oval jumping lane. An oval lane is better than a straight one as the horse is less likely to rush through and one person can work the horse single-handed, whereas, with a straight jumping lane, at least two people are needed, one to start the horse and the other to catch him at the end of the lane. With an oval lane, the trainer simply walks round in the centre and keeps the horse going with the lunge whip.

The jumping lane must not be too big, or the trainer will have trouble keeping the horse going. Nor must it be too small, or there will be no possibility of the horse getting a straight approach to any fence. I have seen horses trained in a circular jumping lane, and they

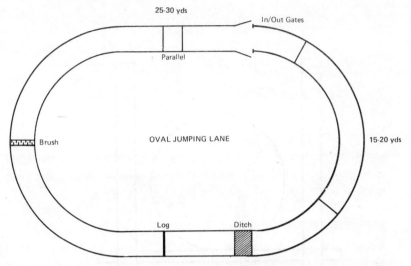

Oval jumping lane in diagram form

were certainly very supple and agile, but work on a continuous circle is strenuous, and the young horses lose impulsion very easily on the circle.

An arena about twenty-five to thirty yards long and fifteen to twenty yards wide will be quite big enough. The track where the jumps will be set should be ten to twelve feet wide. There should be a continuous fence, perferably six to eight feet high, round the outside of the oval, and either a continuous fence (which need not be so high as the outside one) or a partial fence, or sheep hurdles, on the inside of the track. Continuous fencing on the inside makes the trainer's job easier, but once a horse gets the idea of the jumping lane, he will; usually enjoy it so much that there isn't much problem with running out past the jumps.

The fences

The fences (jumps) in the lane should be solid, and as varied as possible, and the heights must be easily adjustable. Solid fences encourage good, clean jumping from the start, and horses seem to know instinctively whether a jump is solid or not. Equally, they know if a fence is insubstantial, and nothing encourages careless jumping so much as training over poorly built, flimsy fences.

It is a good idea to include at least one ditch in the lane. This

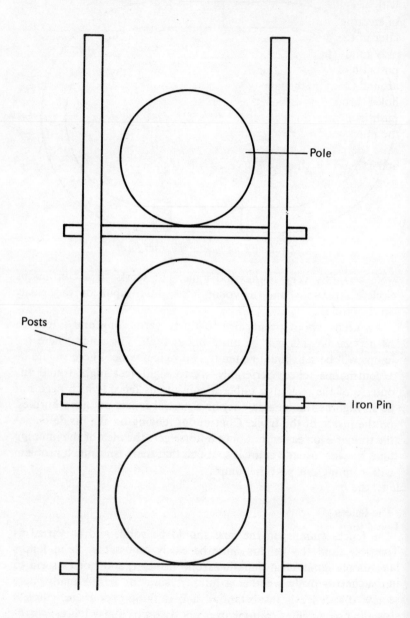

Adjustable jump standard

need not be particularly deep or wide, but should be properly built with sleepers to reinforce the sides. There should be the possibility of erecting parallel rails, for width, and an in-and-out, for use a little later in the horse's training.

A good method of holding the poles in place is to sink two upright posts on each side of the track, about six inches apart, at the places around the jumping lane where you may want to erect a fence. Bore holes through both posts at intervals of about six inches, and then push iron pins through both posts. The jumping poles will rest on the pins, between the two posts, and to increase the height, simply raise the pole and the iron pin to the hole above, or add more pins and poles. The more pairs of upright posts around the jumping

Lungeing over a fence

lane, the more varied you will be able to make your exercises.

Loose jumping

The very first time you send your horse round the loose jumping lane, there should be no fences in it at all. Proceed exactly as described in the chapter on Loose Schooling, and allow the horse to go round several times in both directions. To change direction, you should stop the horse and take him out of the lane and reverse him before starting again in the opposite direction. There would be plenty of room for the horse to turn round inside the lane, even if it is only nine or ten feet wide, but it is better not to encourage him to do this, in case he should decide to reverse himself without being asked.

When the horse has been round the lane without any jumps in it, and is thoroughly confident and happy going round in trot and canter, you may introduce one or two jumps. The jumps should be very low at first, not more than a foot high, and solid looking, with a good ground line. Gradually raise the jumps over a period of two or three weeks, until they are about two feet to two feet six inches, and introduce at least one spread, starting at about two feet wide and gradually increasing it to four and a half feet.

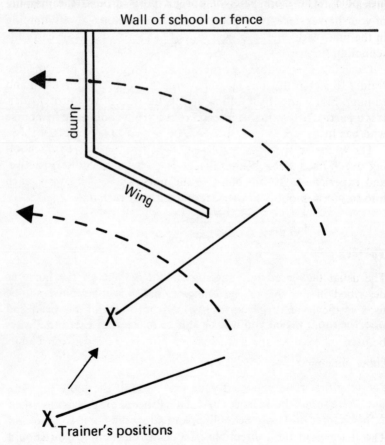

Wall of school or fence

Jump

Wing

X

X Trainer's positions

Lungeing over a jump

Relative positions of trainer, horse and jump

Send the horse round two or three times, until he is going calmly and jumping well, in stride, then stop him quietly and reward him, and send him round the other way. You will find that the horse's balance improves very rapidly and he will become more eager in his ridden work, too.

Lungeing over fences

Lungeing over fences is also a useful exercise. If you have nowhere to construct a loose jumping arena, learn to lunge over jumps instead. Lungeing over fences may be continued throughout the life of your horse, since it is a good way to teach a horse about jumping in the first place, and also a good way to correct faults or carry his schooling further.

Lungeing over fences has the added advantage of allowing the trainer to watch the horse throughout every phase of the jump and to jump him without subjecting him to the added weight of a rider. It is a particularly valuable method of restoring confidence in a horse who has lost it.

The young horse will gain nearly all the advantages of loose schooling over jumps when being lunged, provided the trainer is active, and experienced. It will improve the horse's impulsion and teach him to jump smoothly, in-stride, and without rushing.

The tack

The usual tack used for lungeing should be put on the horse as described in the chapter on lungeing, but side-reins must not be used as they would prevent the horse from lowering his head and making use of his neck and back. Boots or bandages should always be used, at least on the front legs, to protect the legs from bumps and bruises and the possibility of a blow starting up a splint.

The lungeing fence

The fence used for lungeing should have one end close up to a wall in the indoor school, or, if you are working outside, close up to a hedge or fence. At the other side of the jump there should be a wing, consisting of a long pole with one end on the ground and the other end on top of the upright supporting the jump. This is so that the lunge line will slide freely up the pole as the horse jumps and cannot become caught or entangled on any part of the jump. You sometimes see people lungeing a horse over a fence without this wing and they are obliged to raise the lunge line by swinging it up into the air just at the moment the horse jumps. This practice should be avoided at all cost since the sudden movement of the lunge line causes the horse to raise his head and neck over the fence instead of lowering and stretching it.

Start out with no jump at all between the uprights and then lunge the horse quietly, near the uprights, but not going through them at first, in walk and trot. When the horse is going freely in trot with good rhythm, gradually move forward, towards the jump, and allow the horse to make a slightly larger circle which will bring him beyond the wing and between the uprights. Do not be surprised if the horse increases speed, or shies, at first as he goes through between the uprights. Do not get excited, or wave your whip, or frighten him in any way, but, if you feel he is reluctant to go forward, drop a little further behind him so that you are in a stronger driving position.

Early lessons

When the horse is going calmly and correctly between the uprights, in both directions, you may add a pole on the ground and gradually build your jump until it is about a foot high. Remember to change your 'wing' pole each time you change direction, and to work equally on the right and left rein.

Gradually, you will be able to raise the fence, up to about two feet six inches, and add to it to vary it and make it into a spread. Spreads are particularly valuable in the development of the correct muscles, and in teaching the horse to jump using his hocks.

If you have never lunged over fences, start out by practising with an old and experienced horse and make sure you yourself can do it well before trying to lunge a young, green horse over fences. Always take care that the horse has complete freedom of his head and neck over the fence, and that you do not jerk him back immediately on landing. It is natural for the horse to land moving faster forward, probably he will land in canter even if you trot the fence, and you must bring him quietly and gently back to trot, avoiding a sudden jerk on the rein immediately he lands.

Work in trot

Lungeing over fences should be done in trot. Trotting over small jumps develops correct use of the hindquarters far more accurately than jumping at canter. It also avoids the possibility of over-exciting the horse and starting him rushing, while allowing the trainer to keep up the impulsion with the aid of the whip. Later on in the horse's jumping training there is a place for cantering over fences on the lunge, but at this stage using trot is more valuable. If he canters the last stride before a fence, however, do not try to interfere or stop him, as it is too late for him to make any further adjustment and you will only distract his attention and may put him off balance.

Using long-reins

Long-reining over fences is also a good exercise, especially for a horse who becomes excited when jumping on the lunge, since it allows the trainer a great deal more control over the pace and rhythm.

Do not attempt to long-rein over fences until you are thoroughly proficient on the flat. It takes considerable skill to long-rein correctly and until you acquire that skill there is always a danger of either you or the horse becoming entangled in the reins. When you do long-rein over fences, always have the inside rein coming directly to your hand, do not pass it through the stirrup iron on the inside. This allows for more freedom of the horse's head and neck during the jump, which is most important.

Basic objectives

In loose jumping, lungeing or long-reining over fences, always keep your basic objectives in mind. You want your horse to gain confidence, to learn obedience, and to increase his athletic ability through gymnastic exercises. Do not try to do too much too quickly, and always make sure that the lessons are enjoyable and encouraging for your young horse.

10 *Improving Balance, Suppleness and Obedience*

Objectives of first year's training

As your young horse matures and gains in strength, you should become more demanding of him. Provided he is at least four years old you can now continue his elementary training with the object of making him even more supple and obedient, improving his balance and teaching him to respond instinctively to simple aids. This stage will probably last about a year.

By the end of this period the horse should be moving straight and freely forwards, with an even cadence. He should accept a light contact with the bit at all paces, and through transitions and changes of direction. He should jump small, varied fences from trot and canter, alone or in company, without excitement. He should be a good hack, with pleasant manners, and he may be taken out hunting for short days.

As your horse progresses in his training, you do not stop using the exercises you have been using in the past. In fact, all the previous training should be continued, but a higher standard of obedience and a better performance should be demanded of the horse. In addition, you may now move on to some more demanding exercises.

Accepting contact

Teaching your horse to accept, and indeed to seek, a contact with the bit, should be first done in trot. If you attempt it at walk there is the danger that you will artificially raise the horse's head, hollow his back, and get him going behind the bit. Start by walking with a very long rein around your school. Your horse will soon stretch his head and neck forward and down towards the ground, thus lengthening and stretching the muscles of the back and neck.

When he is walking actively, with neck well stretched down, 'suggest' to him that he trot. Do not pick up the rein, but allow the horse to move forward into trot with his head low and the rein loose.

Rise to the trot and after a few moments, very gradually and quietly pick up the reins until you have a light, constant contact with the bit. Done properly, the horse will scarcely raise his head at first, but will continue trotting freely forward, lengthening, but not speeding up, his strides.

Difficulties

Do not expect everything to go exactly right the first time you try this. Probably your horse will try to run quickly in trot the moment you 'suggest' that he trots. If this happens you must quickly and quietly pick up the rein and bring him back to walk and try again. Or perhaps he will walk about for ages waving his head in the air and refuse to lengthen his neck, even on a loose rein. Or maybe he will be the sluggish type and you feel he needs more than a 'suggestion' from you to send him forward into trot.

Whatever your particular difficulty, persevere for a few days and you will be amazed how quickly your horse learns this simple exercise of lengthening his neck and maintaining a long neck and back as you pick up the contact. The time you spend on this lesson will be repaid to you with interest all the life of your horse. He will never forget it and after any period of work in his later training, he will automatically stretch out his back and neck and follow the bit as you yield the rein to him. You may be certain, if you use this method of starting a horse going on contact, that his muscles will grow and develop in the right way.

Some horses are sluggish in their reaction to the rider's aids and it is important that you teach your horse right from the start that he must move forward from the very lightest use of your legs. This is done with the aid of a whip used just behind the leg and immediately following the light leg aid. The horse responds instantly to the whip, you then halt him and re-apply the light leg aid getting the same instant response. Be careful not to frighten the horse, simply make sure that he respects you, your legs and your whip and obeys promptly when given a signal to move. The sequence of the aids is always—light, strong, and immediately light again.

Developing muscles

For muscles to grow and develop they must receive nourishment, by way of a free supply of blood, and work. If the muscles are cramped, by being forced into artificial positions, they cannot be supplied with blood, and therefore cannot receive nourishment and grow.

The amount of work required by any horse at any stage of training is something that experience will teach you, but a book cannot. At first, I would suggest that less harm is done by too little work than too much, so if you are in doubt, stop work sooner rather than later. If you tire the horse's muscles beyond a certain point, lactic acid will build up very rapidly and instead of the muscle being developed by the exercises, it will actually be degenerating.

Watch your horse closely as he works and as he is at liberty. Try to turn him out into a grassy field for at least an hour every day. Not only will this give him an opportunity to eat 'something succulent' each day, but also it will give you a chance to watch him at liberty. A young horse should be full of life and playfulness. He may not dash around a great deal—that will depend on his temperament, but he should be obviously happy, confident and feeling good, particularly on a brisk, sunny morning in spring or autumn.

Suppling exercises

As your periods of mounted work increase in length, you should introduce some more demanding exercises in the form of circles, turns and serpentines. Always start your work period with at least ten minutes of walk and trot on a long rein. Then establish a quiet, active trot with a long neck and gradually pick up your contact. Maintain the contact and move onto a large circle.

If you use one half of the average sized indoor school (one half the length, the full width) you will be on a circle of about seventy feet in diameter. At first you must ride your circle using mainly the inside rein to teach the horse to bend round the track of the movement. The outside hand must yield slightly to allow the horse to stretch the muscles on the outside of his body. Gradually, as the horse becomes better balanced and more supple, you should keep a little more contact with the outside rein, until ultimately, you ride your horse round circles with the inside leg driving him onto the outside rein the inside rein giving only the slightest flexion and the outside leg preventing the quarters from swinging out and therefore ensuring that the inside rein is, in fact, effective all through the length of the horse, including the joints of the inside hind leg. This ultimate result takes many months to achieve and you should not attempt to hurry things along by "forcing" the horse to accept more drive onto the outside rein.

One of the biggest mistakes most people make at this stage is going too fast. Trainers seem to become obsessed by the fear of "loosing impulsion" and then start to confuse impulsion with speed. Remember that difficulties are ironed out much more easily at a slower pace, so concentrate at first on maintaining a very strict rhythm but a very slow pace, without much impulsion. When the horse is more muscled and supple it will be quite easy to develop the necessary impulsion and if you keep things slow at first the horse will remain relaxed and calm instead of becoming tense and excited and setting up resistance to his rider.

Riding loops and turns

When the horse is going well on large circles both to the left and the right and can change his bend in a stride or two across the centre of the school and execute correct large figures of eight, using the whole school, you can introduce shallow loops and turns. Turns are usually performed, at this stage, across the school from one long side to the opposite long side, where the horse is asked either to make a second turn in the same direction as the first turn, or to make the second turn in the opposite direction. The important thing to remember is that the horse must maintain his rhythm and not shorten his stride through the turns. His whole body must be bent in the direction of the turn and he must not be allowed to cut across the corners.

Loops are particularly helpful since they can be performed at first along the long side of the arena and may be quite shallow and will therefore allow the rider time to change the bend of the horse a little bit at a time. Riding loops and turns, be careful to yield a little with the outside hand at first and to maintain the energy and activity of the horse's stride with the action of your inside leg.

The two most common faults are shortening of the stride, which is usually accompanied by the raising and perhaps tilting of the head, and failure to curve the horse's whole body around the track of the movement. If you have no mirrors, or are uncertain of whether your horse is actually curving round the correct track, get a friend to watch you, keeping an eye particularly on these two points. Often, when you are riding a young horse, your attention may be concentrated on one aspect of what you are doing, so that until you become very experienced it is difficult to think of everything all at once and a second pair of eyes observing the results you are getting can be very helpful.

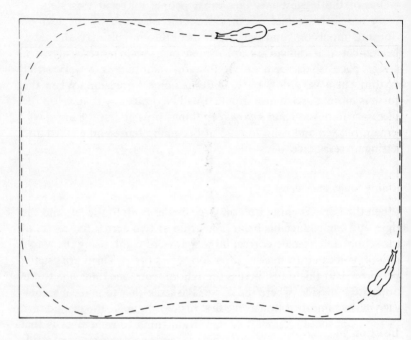

Shallow loops away from the wall

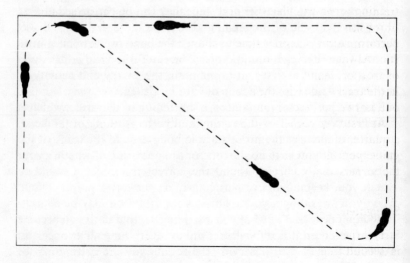

Changing the rein across the diagonal and using the corners

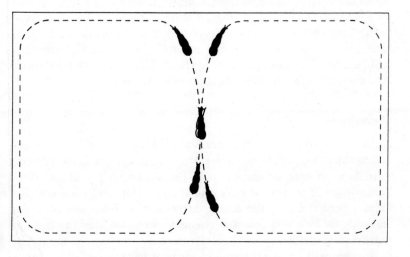

Turning across the school and changing direction

Insist on good performance

With this thought of curving your horse around the track of the movement in mind, remember that every circuit you make of your training arena can be either very beneficial to your horse's training, or positively harmful, depending on how you make your horse perform. Always keep a steady, active rhythm, never let your horse run. Always bend him round every corner, whether you are in walk or trot, or, later in canter, make sure that the hind feet truly follow in the track of the appropriate front foot. The quarters must not fall out, nor be pushed too far in, as is so commonly seen in canter.

At first your corners will be quite shallow arcs—each corner being a quarter of a circle and at this stage your circles are very large. As a guide, you should see the lashes of the inside eye as you pass through the corners.

Straightening the horse

Straightness is another of your objectives at this stage of training. It is difficult to get a young horse straight for a very simple anatomical reason. Horses are narrower through the shoulders than through the hips. Most riders line up the outside of the horse's body along the wall of their arena, and believe that they are straight, when, in fact, the quarters are being carried slightly in. Making large, shallow, loops inwards off the long wall will help you with this problem of straightening the horse and will also counteract his dependence on the wall. Another valuable, and surprisingly difficult exercise, is to ride the horse round the arena on the INSIDE track so that neither the horse nor the rider have the support of the wall.

Transitions

Transitions are the key to success at this stage. It is through transitions that we supple the horse longitudinally, gradually teaching him how to balance himself with the added weight of the rider. Transitions from trot to walk and then to halt, and back into trot again, performed on the centre, after turning from one long side towards the opposite one, and changing direction after the halt, are particularly useful.

Remember to make frequent changes of pace as well as direction. Walk, trot, walk, halt, walk, halt, walk, trot, and so on. This will not only help to keep your horse attentive and teach him to respond to your lightest aid quickly and willingly, but will greatly improve his balance, since all transitions are longitudinal suppling exercises which require the use, and thus development of, the long muscles of the neck, back and quarters.

11 *First Steps in Canter*

When your work in trot on loops, turns and circles is going well, and you have progressed to the stage of being able to bend your horse around the track of the circle, it is time to introduce mounted work at the canter. In fact, canter work should really start as soon as the horse is obedient at trot and responds to your aids.

Cantering in a confined space

It is just as well to teach your horse to strike off on the correct lead at canter right from the start. If you have been riding him outside, you may already have cantered on a long rein on straight lines, but cantering in the school, on command, and maintaining canter round the relatively confined area of the indoor or outdoor manege, demands much more suppleness and balance from your horse.

The aids and trasitions

The first lesson in canter will be on a large circle at one end of the school, or in a corner of a field where you have a fence or hedge on two sides at least. Establish an active, but fairly slow trot, with a good contact, on the circle. When you have balanced the horse round the circle and he is active and attentive and listening to you, sit to the trot, slightly increase the contact with the inside rein, and, as you come into the corner, bring your outside leg back behind he girth and apply it there at the same moment as you apply your inside leg at the girth.

Your inside rein will bend the horse slightly in the direction of the circle and the outside rein maintains a supporting contact to prevent the horse from running in trot. In all probability, if you have good rhythm and have timed your aids correctly, your horse will strike off correctly on the inside lead. If so, continue in canter around the large circle once or twice with a long rein and then bring the horse quietly back to trot by using your seat and leg aids gently to bring his hocks up under him, and restraining his forward movement with a very light hand. The action of the hands should really be nothing more than ceasing to allow the horse to go forward. They should never, in any circumstances, "pull" at the horse's mouth.

At first, to avoid any possibility of the horse throwing his head up in the downward transitions from canter, it is a good idea to use only the inside rein, and that very lightly indeed, combined with your voice aids, and to allow the horse to have his balance more on the forehand than will be the case later on when he is more balanced and supple.

Correcting a wrong lead

If, when you ask for the canter, the horse strikes off on the wrong lead, bring him quietly back to trot and try again. If the horse does not canter at all, but tries to rush forward in a fast trot, stop trying to canter, slow the trot, make some trot, walk, halt, transitions on the circle, and then go back to the trot–canter transitions when the horse is completely calm and relaxed.

Stiffness

If your horse canters willingly on one lead, but simply refuses to take the other lead, it is an indication of extreme stiffness and unbalance, and would also indicate that your preliminary work has not been carried out properly. But there is one method I use sometimes with a spoiled horse brought in for re-training which seldom fails to induce the horse to strike off in canter on the lead he doesn't like. Place a pole on the ground, in the tack, just before the first corner. Trot round the circle and give the horse the aid to canter just as you reach the pole. If your timing is right he will land over the pole in canter on the inside lead. You should have an assistant, if possible, to pull the pole in off the track so that you can continue round the circle once or twice in canter without having to go over it a second time, as there is always the danger that the horse may change leads again in the air as he goes over the pole.

Occasionally, you will come across a horse who is so short-coupled, or is so unsupple, that he canters disunited, or constantly switches leads, either behind only, or both in front and behind. If, after reasonable efforts have been made on the large circle, you are still not obtaining a satisfactory canter, stop asking for canter inside the arena or on the circle until you have worked for some weeks longer at suppling, balancing exercises in trot. Stick to cantering this stiff horse outside, in long straight lines, preferably on slightly uphill gradients. You will find that this exercise improves his gaits and increases his suppleness and confidence in his own ability to keep his balance in canter. You may also find it useful to return to the long-reins and repeat the canter work on long-reins for a week or so before asking for canter in a confined space when mounted.

Cantering in the open

It is a very good idea, when cantering outside, to determine which lead you wish to strike off on and to ask the horse for that lead. Then allow him to canter across a whole field and ask for the other lead through the next field.

Transitions

It is very important to make all transitions and changes of direction smoothly, with good rhythm and maintaining the activity of the hind legs and the length of the horse's stride.

The horse's head should not be thrown up as he makes downwards transitions, particularly from canter to trot. To avoid this head throwing you must be very gentle with your hands. Train your horse to listen to your seat and legs by preceeding every aid, particularly aids for downward transitions, by sitting deep in your saddle and closing your thighs slightly so that your seat ceases to follow the movement of the horse. Very quickly your horse will associate this pressure and the lack of a following seat, with the transition which follows, and he will balance himself automatically, bringing his hocks more deeply underneath him when he feels the holding and restraining of your seat.

'Using' the back

It is a mistake to sit 'heavily' on a young horse's back, or to attempt to exert very strong driving aids with your seat and back, as there is a danger of hollowing your horse's back. However, the horse is very sensitive and you will be surprised how quickly he will learn to balance himself under you whenever you 'sit deep', as described above, on him.

If you are not sure about how hard to use your back and how

strongly you should drive with your seat, try just a very little pressure at a time. Remember that the 'lightest possible aid' is what you are seeking. Any time you feel your horse hollow his back out under you, or raise his head, you know you have gone too far or you are not applying your aids correctly. Most often this is the result of the rider gripping with the thigh and using too strong a hand.

What you should feel is the hind legs coming under you, the head and neck reaching forward and down, the back coming up very slightly under you, and the whole horse 'filling out' between your legs. The more sensitive you can teach yourself to become to the feel of what your horse is doing underneath you, the more supple and light and well schooled your young horse is going to become.

Common faults and difficulties

The most common faults which occur when teaching a horse to canter are "rushing" the horse into a canter through a fast, running trot; and trying to 'throw' the horse onto the inside lead by pulling his head to the outside and unbalancing him. Both these mistakes can be avoided if the rider will think ahead and take the time to balance the young horse at trot before asking for a canter strike off.

At this stage the canter should always be obtained through trot and not straight from the walk, since the horse will be too much on his forehand, with the added and unaccustomed weight of the rider, to make the transition from the walk correctly.

Work your horse in canter equally on both reins. If he finds one direction much harder than the other, then do more of your work on the difficult rein. As with the work at trot, you should work on large circles, wide turns, and many transitions, quietly and smoothly ridden, up and down through trot to walk and halt until the horse becomes relaxed in the work and consistent in striking off on the correct lead both on circles and on the straight. Much of this work should be done on a long rein with only the lightest of contact with the mouth, and some should be done with a completely loose rein, allowing the horse to stretch his neck at will.

12 *Turns on the Forehand and*
    Leg Yielding

By the time your horse has completed all the work in the previous chapters, he is ready to learn about moving away from the rider's leg. The turn on the forehand, which is a useful and practical move-ment enabling the rider to place the horse accurately for such manoeuvres as opening gates, is the first exercise generally used to accomplish this.

The turn on the forehand

In the turn on the forehand, the horse's hind legs describe a circle around his front legs. The inside front leg is the 'pivoting' leg. It must be picked up and put down on the same spot three or four times during each half turn. In the right turn on the forehand, the right hind leg crosses in front of the left hind and the right front is the pivoting leg. The whole horse must be slightly curved in the direction of the turn, so that the rider can just see the corner of his eye. In the case of the right turn on the forehand the body of the horse is slightly curved right, around the rider's inside leg. The horse must not be allowed to step back. This exercise should increase the horse's impulsion and lighten his forehand, because it makes the hind-quarters more active and supple. Every turn on the forehand should be immediately followed by foreward movement.

Preparation for the turn

Do not attempt the turn on the forehand until your horse will come to a square, balanced halt, and stand still, without resistance. Then ask only one or two steps at a time and move forwards. To make a right turn on the forehand: bring the horse to a square halt, feel the right rein and apply the right leg slightly behind the girth in a series of rhythmic squeezes. The left leg remains close to the horse, ready

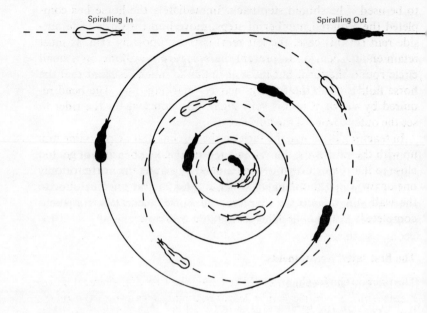

Improving balance and impulsion; spiraling in and out on the circle

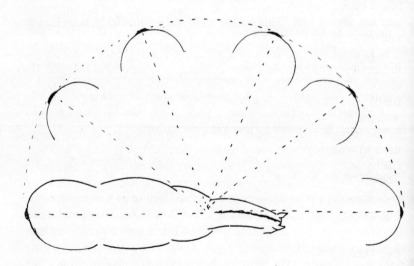

Turn on the forehand

to be used if he should step back. Immediately the horse has completed the required number of steps, move him forwards. The outside rein (in this case, the left rein) is the supporting rein. It must retain enough tension to prevent the horse from walking on a small circle round the turn, but must not offer so much restraint that the horse fails to keep the forelegs actively marking time. The bend required by the right rein is very slight, just sufficient for the rider to see the outer corner of the horse's eye.

In teaching the horse the turn on the forehand, it helps to line him up with the side of the school, or a fence or hedge, but do not get too close to it at first since you want to start by asking the horse for only one or two steps and then walk forwards. If you are lined up close to the wall you will not be able to do this, but will have to make a complete half turn of 180° before you can go forwards.

The first lateral movements

The turn on the forehand could be called the first of the lateral movements, since the horse is now learning to step away from the rider's leg. Most young horses understand what is required with little difficulty and soon become proficient at the turn on the forehand, but if you have difficulty getting the horse to step away from your leg, ask a friend to stand beside the horse and touch his hindleg, just below the hock, with a series of light taps in rhythm with the leg aid you are giving him. This added whip aid will quickly help him to understand what you want him to do.

It is quite normal for the horse to step away easily and almost instinctively on one side, and to be a little more resistant to the opposite leg. This is simply his natural one-sidedness showing up and should only be a problem for a day or two, if tackled calmly and with the help of someone on the ground.

The turn on the forehand is not a classical movement. It is simply used to teach the horse to step away from the rider's leg, and once the horse has mastered this it should not be practised. Another such exercise, which is used in some countries as a stepping stone to the shoulder-in, and which is purely a means to the end of teaching the horse to react correctly to the aids of the rider's leg, is 'leg yielding'.

Leg yielding

In fact, there are two types of leg yielding—inside leg yielding, and outside leg-yielding. Let us start by considering outside leg yielding.

In outside leg yielding the horse is made to travel forwards and sideways at the same time. His outside hindleg crosses in front of his inside hindleg, his body is kept straight with just the slightest inclination of his head to the direction he is going. The outside foreleg will also cross slightly in front of the inside foreleg.

The best place to start teaching this movement to the horse is along the long side of the school, or, if you are outside, along a fence or hedge. Once the horse has mastered the movement it may be performed anywhere in the school, for instance, across the diagonal. But do remember that it is simply a means to the end of teaching the horse to move away from the rider's leg and that once this end is achieved you will gain much more benefit from the classical movements of shoulder-in and half pass and you should no longer practise leg yielding.

First attempts

To achieve the best result at the start of this lesson in leg yielding, warm up your horse at walk and trot in the usual way and perform some large circles in trot, figures of eight, and upward and downward transitions. Then bring your horse to an active walk, with a steady contact and slightly shortened stride, round the short end of the school. Let us assume that you are on the right rein, travelling clockwise around the arena. As you come away from the short side into the long side of the arena, cut the corner so that your horse is almost straight on a diagonal line across the corner. Draw your outside leg (the left leg in this case) back slightly behind the girth and apply it in a series of short squeezes, assisted, if necessary, at first by small taps from your whip behind your left leg. Your right leg stays in position, close to the horse, ready to use if the horse loses forward movement. Your left rein is a supporting rein and prevents the horse from turning to the right, and the right rein leads the horse down the track. In fact, the tension on both reins should be equal.

The position of the rider is most important. Sit squarely in the centre of your saddle and do not allow yourself to lean over in either direction. The tendency is for the rider to lean to the left in attempting to leg yield to the right, but this is completely unnecessary. Use your legs softly and in rhythm and avoid any tendency to jerk your body from the hips or shoulders.

Correct angle and head position

At first, the angle of the horse to the wall should be very slight, and never more than 30°. A larger angle will tend to restrict forward movement. You will find that, due to the position of the horse's eyes, on the side of his head, it is easier to have the head flexed very slightly towards the direction of the movement—in this case, to the right— since if the head is kept dead straight in front of the body the presence of the wall will tend to stop the free forward movement of the horse, but this flexion should be very slight, and the horse should be kept as near straight as possible.

Practise leg yielding in walk, at first, and only ask for a few steps at a time. After the horse has taken two or three steps, apply your inside leg (in the case of leg yielding to the right, this would be your right leg) and send him actively forward in the track. Naturally, you should practise the movement equally to the right and the left.

As soon as your horse has understood what is required and performs the movement fairly well in walk, practise it in sitting trot. It goes without saying that before you attempt to train a young horse you must be a fairly proficient rider, and you should certainly be able to ride any horse comfortably at sitting trot, keeping a good position and very steady legs and hands without gripping. The reason for moving the horse into trot as soon as possible is to maintain plenty of forward movement. With any lateral work there exists always the danger of losing free forward movement and it is easier to maintain impulsion in trot than it is in walk.

Bending the horse

Inside leg yielding is that bending of the horse's body away from the rider's leg which we ask for in every corner or circle we ride. At first you allow a young horse to make very shallow corners as he goes around the arena, but gradually you ask for more and more bend through each corner by asking the horse to yield from your inside leg. To achieve this bending of the horse's body, the rider applies the inside leg at the girth area, combined with the use of the inside rein, slightly in the direction of the outside hip. The outside leg, meanwhile, is drawn slightly back to prevent the horse's quarters from falling out, and the outside rein again acts as the supporting rein. At first, the tension taken on the outside rein will be slight, but as the horse becomes more supple and balanced and begins to come on the bit, the main contact will change from the inside rein to the outside rein, so that eventually you are driving your horse with your inside leg into your outside hand.

The yielding of the horse's body away from the rider's inside leg is a most important factor in the achievement of truly round circles. Until the horse has mastered this inside leg yielding he will not follow a truly circular track, but will make a series of short straight lines at a tangent to the circle.

Importance of preparation

Although it is claimed by many experts that leg yielding may be performed without any collection, and that is why it is a suitable preliminary exercise for use at this stage of the horse's training as a preparation to shoulder-in and half-pass, I must stress that it should not be attempted without suitable preparation. The horse should be prepared by warming up exercises in walk and trot, and by upward and downward transitions, and before being asked to attempt leg yielding he should be at least "put together" in an active walk by the combined driving action of the rider's legs and the restraining action of the fingers. Particularly for outside leg yielding, his body should be positioned in such a way as to make the exercise easy for him, but at the same time demanding that he use his hind legs properly and really start to bend the joints of the haunches.

Always follow the work at leg yielding with active forward movement in trot. It is a good moment to start asking the horse for a slightly lengthened stride in trot, using the increased activity of the hind legs produced by the leg yielding, but again remember to ask for only a few steps at a time, and do not continue to drive forwards if the horse starts to 'run' taking shorter, faster steps instead of slightly longer ones.

As usual, finish your training session with a walk on a long rein so that the horse can thoroughly stretch and relax all his neck and back muscles.

Simple Change of Lead at Canter

Awareness of Rhythm

Looking back over the past few chapters I am surprised to see how little I have mentioned rhythm. Rhythm and feel are two vitally important aspects of the training, or retraining, of any horse. Perhaps I haven't mentioned rhythm much just because it is so much a part of riding at all times that it should be as impossible for a horse-man to ride in bad rhythm as it would be for a musician to play his music that way. Our horses are our instruments and we should always aim to produce from them a performance of rhythmic, graceful beauty.

Every horse has his own ideal rhythm. The tempo of the footfalls varying slightly from one horse to another and the natural length of the stride varying quite considerably between one horse and another. The stage of basic training which occupies the first serious year of mounted work, that is, from four to five, is concerned mainly with teaching the horse to move freely and actively forward, straight, with good rhythm, and improving his balance, suppleness and obedience to the aids. During this period of his training the horse will also learn to lengthen and stretch his neck and back, and to develop a long, roomy stride whilst carrying the rider's weight on his back.

Riding to music

To help improve the horse's rhythm I very often ride to music. Since it is sometimes difficult to find the kind of music I like on the radio, I have a record player in the indoor school and records of Mozart, Vivaldi, Bach and Verdi. Almost any music that you happen to like, provided it is not terribly fast or terribly slow, is suitable for riding to and will help you to develop good rhythm in your riding.

Many people working on their own have difficulty finding the right tempo for their horses. Some rush madly about the arena because they are afraid of 'losing impulsion' and so they never really allow their horses to develop the full scope of their stride at any gait, particularly at trot. It is better to go too slowly at first, *without* sufficient impulsion, to allow the horse time to think and the rider time to feel what's going on, than to rush round performing a series of meaningless movements. It is amazing how easily some apparently difficult problems can be ironed out if the rider will just slow down.

Changing the tempo

Try it. Ride on a large circle at rising trot. Start out at whatever pace you usually ride at. Then slow the horse down, not by using pressure of the reins, but by deliberately slowing down your rising and not rising so high out of the saddle. Your horse will slow down and take his rhythm from you.

This is exactly what you must do throughout your training. *You* set the rhythm, in your head. It should be pulsating through you, the rhythm of the correct trot, for example, and if you are having difficulty getting a really round circle, or keeping the horse relaxed and on the bit, deliberately slow your rhythm down and go very slowly at first. When the shape and the feel of the horse is exactly right, then increase your impulsion by first slightly increasing the tempo in your head and secondly applying a stronger driving aid through your back, seat and lower leg, if necessary.

Changing the lead at canter

The question of correct rhythm becomes particularly important when we start to consider changes at the canter. At this stage we are thinking of simple changes of lead, through trot. In the "dressage" sense, a 'simple change' involves going from canter to walk, and back into canter again on the opposite lead. But to perform the change through walk at this stage of training would probably put the young horse behind the bit, so we will ask simply for a canter, trot, canter transition.

Preparation

The best way to prepare for changes at the canter is to work on a large circle, taking up one complete half of your school or manege. Practise transitions from canter to trot, and after ten or twelve trot strides go back into canter again for seven or eight strides, then back to trot again, and so on. This exercise can, in fact, be done on a long, almost loose rein, but if you are preparing to teach your horse the simple change of lead, you should be riding with a contact and the horse well balanced and "together".

Transitions leading to changes

When the horse will perform the downward and upward transitions on the circle quietly, calmly and accurately, with good rhythm, coming from the canter immediately into a good, two-beat trot and then off into canter again with no fuss, he is ready to try a change. Bring him to trot as you approach the centre of the school, and instead of continuing round the track of your circle at one end, change the bend of the horse in trot as you cross the centre and, start out to describe a circle in the opposite direction at the other end of your manege. Provided the horse is quiet and balanced, stay in trot only five or six strides, and then ask for a strike off in canter on the new lead.

Continue circling the full width of the school on the new lead, and proceed with the exercise of cantering round the circle making several transitions from canter to trot and back to canter again, making sure that the horse performs in a balanced, supple manner, in good rhythm. If the horse is calm and obedient, make another simple change in the centre.

Anticipating and rushing

If you find that your horse is perhaps a little over-active and antici- pates the changes, particularly from trot into canter, or if he has a tendency to rush or bound into the canter, be careful not to overdo your work at transitions at first. Allow the horse to stay in canter on one lead for a longer period, making a complete circuit of the school, then perhaps a large circle at one end, then going down the long side and turning up the centre line and away in the same direction, and so on, before returning to your work at smooth transitions on the circle and changes of lead. If the over-excitement persists, bring the horse quietly to a walk on a long rein and continue to walk until he is absolutely calm, then try again.

Correct rhythm

Another problem which arises fairly frequently is an inability to get a good trot rhythm immediately after the canter. This is very

important and is simply a question of improving your riding. Insist
that the horse comes from the canter into an onward moving trot
with a perfect two beats and concentrate hard enough to accomplish
this. In this case, of course, as it would be meaningless to canter
round and round the ring on one lead, you should make very
frequent transitions to trot and back into canter again.

Varying the placing of the changes

When you can achieve good simple changes through trot using the
large figure of eight, try making the change on a loop. For example,
canter on the right lead down one long side and around the short
end and then canter across the diagonal, aiming well before the
quarter marker. Bring the horse to trot somewhere shortly after X,
balance the trot and just as you bend onto the short side on the left
rein, strike off in canter on the left lead. This is an excellent exercise,
but beware of the horse learning to anticipate a change. Sometimes
you should not ask for the canter on the new lead but should ask
instead for a halt, followed by moving forward in trot again on the
circle, or simply ask for a trot circle using half the school instead of
asking the horse to canter on round the track again.

Finally, you perform the simple change on the straight line. The
easiest way to start this is to ask for the change on the diagonal, at X.
Later on you can ask for the change on the quarter line. Canter
round the school on the right rein, come to a trot on the short end
and turn down the quarter line, leaving plenty of room between you
and the wall on your left. As soon as you are through the right
handed corner, position your horse a little to the left, and being
very distinct with your left leg at the girth and right leg and shoulder
slightly back, ask for the strike off on the left lead. Come back to a
balanced trot before reaching the next short end, as it is still too soon
to ask for counter canter round the short end of the arena.

As with all training, this lesson of making simple changes of lead
at canter must not be hurried. It should not be attempted until fairly
late in this part of the horse's training, and you must allow the horse
plenty of time and practice to master the exercise correctly.

Lateral suppling

Other school exercises which you can usefully use at this stage
include leg-yielding on a large circle, at walk, and reducing and

increasing the perimeter of the circle at trot, by spiralling in and out. The first of these exercises is really a simple 'inside leg-yield' and a preliminary for shoulder-in. Establish a circle, approximately fifteen metres in diameter and at least three metres from the walls of your school. Walk on the circle keeping the horse well balanced, on a contact, with a shortened stride, and 'ask' with the inside leg for the quarters to move two steps off the perimeter of the circle to the outside. Immediately "receive" the quarters with the outside leg and return them to the track of the circle. Do not ask for more than two or three steps at a time and remember that it is important to "straighten" the horse around the track of the circle between each "asking" for a yield from your leg. Throughout, the horse should be slightly bent in the direction in which he is going, i.e. if you are on, the right rein, travelling clockwise, the whole horse should be slightly bent to the right.

The exercise should, of course, be performed equally to each direction. There are many similar exercises which are developed on the circle later, including shoulder-in, haunches-in, and half pass. But be careful at this stage not to overdo work of this nature, which is very concentrated and demands a great deal of effort from the horse, both mentally and physically.

Improving balance

The spiralling exercise in trot on the circle is an excellent way to improve balance, cadence and impulsion. Establish trot on a large circle, twenty metres at least. You will probably get the best results from using the sitting trot. Make sure you do not demand too much from the young horse's back, and do not insist on much impulsion at first. Ask for a relaxed, rhythmic trot, the horse accepting a contact, and the impulsion maintained at an even level throughout the exercise. You will find that the stride gradually shortens and the horse will become more collected and better balanced.

Gradually reduce the perimeter of your circle, following a track which would look something like a coil spring if drawn upon the ground. Make sure that you are really riding round circles and that the horse's hind feet are following directly in the track of his forefeet. This exercise becomes more difficult and demands more bend from the horse and consequently harder work from the inside hind leg as the circles get smaller and smaller. Do not reduce the circle to less than fifteen metres at first, and work towards a circle of ten metres by the end of the year of training. Keep the circles either concentric, that is, you will gradually move inwards away from the walls evenly all around your circle, or based with a fixed point, say at A or C, when you will touch the track at the fixed point each time around, but the circle will reach progressively less and less far from your fixed point. When you have achieved the smallest circle you plan to ask for from your horse, gradually *increase* the size of the circles once again, spiralling out onto the original perimeter.

Take plenty of time over this exercise, do not simply dash in and out from the large to the small circles, and be particularly careful over rhythm throughout.

Riding in the open and Manners

Riding your young horse outside is very important. A young horse constantly ridden in the indoor school or manege may easily become sour, and the very fact of riding outside creates a more natural impulsion. To improve balance, ride up and down hill at all paces. Do not, however, allow the horse to 'run' down the hills, as he will undoubtedly want to do, but hold him quietly in check with your seat and ensure that the trot, or canter, or walk, rhythm remains unchanged, even though the stride may be slightly lengthened due to the downhill slope. Even quite steep hills are good, but take them slowly, and keep the horse straight in order to avoid undue strain on young limbs and back. Riding over ridge and furrow is another excellent balance exercise, and also teaches a horse to look where he is putting his feet.

Now is the time to make sure your young horse will stand to open and close gates, walk through thick, "blind" places, and will walk through water, calmly and quietly. It is a good idea to take along an older stable mate at first, and, of course, only take a young horse through water which has a safe, firm bottom.

Much of your work outside should be on a loose rein, which not only helps the horse to balance himself properly, but also makes him a more pleasant ride. Always insist on good manners, alone, with company, with machines, traffic, dogs, farm animals, etc. Remember that manners are catching, not only between horses, but from rider to horse as well. Stable manners, too, are very important, and are largely a matter of early handling. How much more you will enjoy your horse in the future if you can ensure now that his behaviour is always good.

It goes without saying that if you plan to train your own horse, you must be able to ride at least well enough over fences not to interfere with your horse when he jumps, and to maintain a good position from which to control the horse. If you are in any doubt about your own ability as a rider, you would be well advised to do all the training of your horse under the supervision of a good instructor, or at the very least, to hand over his initial jumping training to a competent rider.

Importance of trotting poles

Your young horse will already have been led over poles on the ground, loose schooled over low fences in a free schooling manege and lunged over small fences. Provided he goes quietly and freely in these circumstances and that he is moving freely forward from your leg aids when ridden on the flat, you may now go ahead with some basic mounted schooling over jumps. From the horse's point of view, this involves adaptating and rebalancing in order to adjust to carrying the weight of the rider, but it should not be a cause of over-excitement or fear.

Once again, rhythm is of vital importance, and it is a good plan to work over trotting poles to develop the necessary rhythm as well as developing the muscles your horse will use in carrying you over a fence.

How to start

Start by walking over a single pole on the ground. Allow your horse to lower his head and look at the pole. In jumping, he will lower his head and neck on the approach to a fence; at take off he will shorten his neck and raise his head, and then, with hocks well under himself, he will lift his forehand off the ground. The next stage of the jump will involve his stretching out his head and neck as he springs upwards and forwards. In suspension, his head and neck will be stretched fully forward and down. His hind legs are then gathered up under his belly and in landing, his head and neck come up, the neck shortens as the forefeet are stretched down to the ground.

Walk over the pole on the ground once or twice, on a large circle, then trot on rising and trot over the pole two or three times in each direction. Have a helper with you and when you have trotted over the pole with the horse relaxed and in good rhythm several times, get your helper to place two more poles on the ground approximately four and a half feet apart. Once again, start by walking through the three poles once or twice until the horse realises that you want him to step between each pole, then, still on the circle, continue in trot. Very seldom does this exercise cause any difficulty if carried out with thoughtful common sense. Provided the horse is trotting through the poles with good rhythm, increase the size of your circle until you are trotting round the whole arena and trotting through the poles, heading straight for the centre of each pole, on a straight line.

Over-keenness

If you do have any difficulties, they will probably be caused by the horse being over-keen. In this case, slow everything down by using your seat, rising slower and less high, and remain on the circle so that the horse is on a continuous curve. A circle tends to reduce a horse's natural impulsion, whereas a straight line tends to increase it. If the horse doesn't settle and trot through the poles correctly, come back to a walk and start again from there.

Work on both reins equally

Remember how important it is to work equally in both directions, and do not continue the exercise to the point of making the horse bored with it. The correct way for the horse to perform through trotting poles is with increased impulsion, a more active and elevated stride, the head and neck carried a little lower than normal so that the horse can look at the poles and the rider maintaining a quiet, definite contact with the horse's mouth without in any way interfering with it. The rider should rise to the trot all the way through the poles and should be very careful throughout this phase of training not to interfere with the horse's natural movement and enjoyment with either his hands or his weight. It is a good plan for the rider on a green horse to hook one finger through the martingale strap, or to put on a neck-strap to catch hold of, or at least, to hold on to the mane when jumping small fences at first. The horse should enjoy jumping and it is important for the trainer to foster this enjoyment.

The first small fences

After a week or so, when you have established a good rhythm through the trotting poles, add a small jump, no more than 18 inches high, about nine feet from the last trotting pole. Be sure your little jump is directly in line with the trotting poles, and place wings on either side of it.

The difficulties encountered at this stage are almost always due to the rider leaning too far forward or looking down. Trot through the poles at an active pace, but not too fast, looking up well ahead, and rising through the poles. Just before the little jump, sit down and squeeze with both legs. Be sure to hook one finger in the martingale strap and let the reins slip out through your fingers so that there is no possibility of catching the horse in the mouth.

The jump at the end of the trotting poles may gradually be increased to 2 feet 6 inches high, with a spread of three feet. Be sure to practise the exercise equally in each direction, even if it means rebuilding your jump from time to time.

At the same time as you are teaching the horse to go through trotting poles and over a small fence in the manege, you can be riding him over poles or small logs and small ditches outside. After two or three weeks, try two parallel logs, a larger tree trunk, slightly wider ditches, but don't get excited about the jumping and on no account rush your horse about when practicing.

Jumping from the trot

Trot is the best pace at this stage. It is less effort for the horse to jump from trot than to jump from a walk, and it is less exciting than jumping from the canter. At this stage it is better to increase the size of the jumps by widening them rather than by making them higher. In order to jump the necessary width, the horse will jump higher in any case. Jumping from the trot will also teach the horse to use his hocks properly and it will be easy for him to judge his take off.

During the first year of jumping, the jumps should be kept very small indeed, but they should be as varied as possible. A young hunter or eventer should not go beyond three feet six inches in height in his first year of jumping, nor beyond eight feet in width, and a pony should not be asked to jump more than about two feet six inches in height and perhaps four feet in width.

Jumping should be fun

It is at this stage that the horse is 'made' or 'ruined' for life. Jumping must be fun and never associated with pain of any sort. Be particularly careful always to approach jumps with the horse straight between your hand and leg. Make sure you go round the corner before the fence properly, in control of the quarters, which are your engine. Do not ask a young horse to jump fences coming out of the corner, because it is too difficult for him to get round the corner properly and at the same time rebalance himself and jump, so probably he would swing the quarters out to one side and either run out or refuse the jump, or, at best, jump it badly. Nor must you ever catch the horse in the mouth.

Pain in his mouth will not be easily forgotten and there is simply no excuse for ever jerking on the reins when jumping. Even if you have to approach the jump in sitting trot to keep the horse moving straight forwards, you should not jerk on the reins when the horse jumps, but simply allow them to slip through your opened fingers, and pick them up quietly on the landing side.

The landing

The landing side of the fence is just as important as the take off side. After landing, the horse should proceed straight forward and quietly be brought down to a walk and then a halt on a straight line. Too often you see young horses being allowed to land after a fence and turn sharply round in one direction or the other, swinging the quarters around the forehand, in order to rejoin their companions as quickly as possible.

Vary the fences

Although the height and width of the fences should be kept small, there is an endless variety that can be jumped. Jump small banks, walls, coloured poles, wet ditches, dry ditches, blind ditches, cavaletti, easy fences up and down slopes, and easy in and outs.

The importance of jumping ditches cannot be over-emphasised. Of course, when you are outside, it is always a good idea to have an older horse with you as companion/schoolmaster, and at first the young horse should follow the older one, until he has gained sufficient confidence to go on his own, and then he should be asked to jump sometimes beside and sometimes in front of his friend.

Good fence construction

Jumping plenty of spread fences from trot will ensure that the horse is active and developing the necessary muscles, as well as learning to place himself correctly at his fences. Schooling fences should be solid and well built. They should have a wide 'face' and, if they are 'island' fences in the middle of a field, it is a good idea to use wings at first. If a young horse is overfaced at this stage he will quickly learn to refuse instead of developing the habit of jumping whatever he is asked. After all, jumping is simply moving forward in the direction his rider is asking him to go, regardless of the fact that there is a small obstacle in his way.

Take plenty of time

Do not be in a hurry to start jumping at a canter. It is easy to make a horse jump faster but it is quite difficult to stop 'rushing' if it becomes a habit. When you are ready to start jumping fences in canter, begin by working over your trotting poles—three poles is sufficient—then place the first fence nine feet from the last pole and the horse will jump that fence in trot and usually land in canter. Place the second small fence about thirty feet away (more if your horse is big and has a long stride) in a straight line. This will give you two strides in canter after landing from the first jump before jumping the second fence.

When the horse performs this exercise calmly and well, a third fence may be added, either one or two cantering strides beyond the second jump. This jumping along a 'grid' is an excellent gymnastic exercise for both horse and rider, but remember that if your horse is rather 'hot' this may be too exciting for him. If, on the other hand, he doesn't always move sufficiently freely forward, jumping down a 'grid' will help improve his rhythm, balance and activity.

When you are jumping small fences outside in canter, ride the horse hard enough to make him take off well back from his fence, but do not hurry him. He should jump in good style, with a calm and cadenced stride both before and after the jump, and he will, if you prepare him properly and make certain he is kept straight and balanced and moving straight forward between your hand and leg.

You should keep lightly in contact with your horse's mouth during the approach and keep your hands low, still and giving all the time. The horse should not get excited over his jumping, but he should enjoy it.

The young horse may certainly go out with hounds at this stage of his training, preferably with a reliable companion. An hour or two will be sufficient, and he should hilltop rather than hunt. Depending on the time of year, he might also go to one or two beginner shows or hunter trials, providing he is jumping well and in good style, and that he is not entered in any class where the jumps would go beyond three feet. Any or all of these outings will help to keep the horse fresh, alert and interested in life and avoid him becoming bored or sour with work at home in the ring.

15 *More Jumping Exercises*

The jumping training of your young horse should continue side by side with his training on the flat. Good jumping is really about ninety per cent achieved on the flat, not by work over fences at all. But it is very good to vary the work you ask of your horse, and introducing jumping into your weekly schedule will help to keep him fresh and attentive.

How often to jump

Your programme of training is going to depend to some extent on the weather and the state of the ground and whether you have an indoor riding school available. Ideally your weekly programme might be something like this:- Monday—working in the indoor school on suppling exercises, circles, turns, halts, changes of direction. Followed by some work over cavaletti. Tuesday—a hack outside. Make use of the lanes to practice moving the horse away from your leg. Trotting up and down hill, walking through water, etc. Jump any small logs or ditches you can find. Wednesday—working in the school again, this time spending only about twenty minutes on work on the flat and then proceeding with jumping exercises. Thursday—try to work outside again, perhaps working on the flat for half an hour in a corner of a field and then going for a long trot round the fields and then a long slow canter. Again, by all means jump any small obstacles which may be around. Friday—work over a small course of fences after a twenty minute warm up, and Saturday devote to schooling on the flat, with perhaps some cavaletti work at the end, or, alternatively a long trot round the fields at the end, or a walk out on the lanes on a loose rein. Sunday (or at any rate, one day a week) should be a day of rest. If possible turn the horse out for an hour or so, or if this is not possible, then at least lead him out on a halter and allow him to nibble the grass.

It is good practice to give your horse ten minutes' grazing every day, since that bite of fresh green grass will do him more good than all the tonics or vitamins you can buy. Which doesn't mean he won't need a vitamin supplement, he probably does, but you should consult with your Veterinarian about this.

How many jumps to take

At the start of training, when the jumps are very small, you can almost jump an unlimited number of times without harming or tiring the horse, but once the fences reach 3 ft. you must cut down the number of actual jumps considerably. Twelve or so fences is plenty in one session, unless, for instance, you are jumping a small course of, say, eight fences and the first round you do does not satisfy you. Then jump the whole course again, and get it right so that you can finish on a very good note. If it still isn't good enough, select just three or four of the fences and jump them again, and if necessary, yet once more, until you get a really satisfactory couple of fences to finish over. If, on the other hand, the horse has only jumped six or seven obstacles, but has done it very well, in a balanced manner, without rushing or napping or refusing or any other difficulties, then reward him by finishing and taking him out to cool off and then back to his stable.

As with all training, it is easy to overdo jumping and sour the horse by endless repetition. Knowing when to stop is just as important as knowing when you must go on—and possibly more difficult. The horse does learn by repetition, but he also learns by associating a particular action of his with a pleasant and comfortable reaction from his rider. Thus it is a good thing to associate in his mind the pleasant result of stopping work when his action has been a succession of particularly good jumps. I believe that the final jump in any training session is by far the most important one. The memory of this jump, whether it was good or bad, comfortable or not, remains with the horse and exerts the very strongest influence on his training, regardless of what happened earlier in the lesson. So always make sure you finish on a good note.

Suitable jumping exercises

You must always keep in mind exactly what you wish to achieve in each lesson. So far as jumping is concerned, you want the horse to have arrived at a state of self-carriage, so that he can approach his fences balanced and jump easily, off his hocks, without undue strain and without any excitement.

It is a good idea, during your warm-up period before jumping, to trot the horse over one or two small fences. This is especially true if he is inclined to rush. You may trot a fence, either sitting or rising, but for the horse who rushes I recommend sitting. This may sound back to front. You might reasonably suppose that a horse would get less excited in rising trot. However, it is my experience that a horse who rushes gains great confidence from having the rider sit in the saddle with the legs close and quietly active on the approach to a fence. The horse then knows that the rider is still there. Curiously, this type of highly strung horse who often rushes,

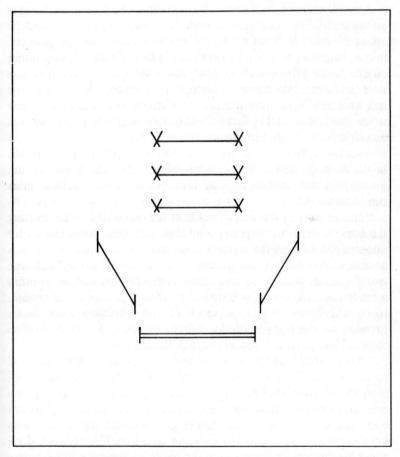

Diagram A: School set up with trotting poles and fence with two small fences on the diagonals

becomes panic stricken if he thinks the rider has gone away. He will feel that the rider is no longer there if the legs are held away from his sides and the rider's back hollowed so that the seat is tipped forward out of the saddle. This is also easily seen in the case of a horse who stops at the last moment. Watch the rider. Nine times out of ten you will notice that he is dropping the reins and falling slightly forward, or looking down, just in front of the fence. The horse feels suddenly deserted, and, not knowing what to do, stops.

You can let the horse have all the rein he wants over the top of the fence, but you must keep the contact on the take off side until he is in the air.

A useful exercise for a horse at this stage is to set up a small jump on the centre line of the school, with three trotting poles, or cavaletti about 6″ high, in front of it. The distance from the last cavaletti to the jump may be anything between 17½ feet and 24 feet, depending on the horse's stride and whether you want him to take a canter stride in front of the fence, or jump it from the trot. With 24 feet he will normally land over the last cavaletti in canter and take one stride and jump. At 17½ feet he will trot through the poles and trot one stride and jump. Either way, this is a very good exercise. If you also set two cavaletti, or small fences on the diagonals, as illustrated in the diagram above, you will be able to keep the horse moving quietly and rhythmically forward throughout a whole exercise series (see diagram A).

You can start by trotting circles at either end of the arena, putting the horse a little bit 'together' and then turn him down the centre line straight through the trotting poles and over the small jump. It is normal to rise through the trotting poles, but by all means sit to the trot if you feel your horse needs the drive from your seat to maintain a really good rhythm. If you do sit, make sure you are good enough to sit with a supple and relaxed back and a constant, very light, pressure on the reins, no jerking of your hands. To teach a horse to jump you must develop very sympathetic hands.

After jumping the fence on the centre, proceed straight forward to the end of the school and then turn right. Go round the school then the quarter marker beyond your original starting point, and turn and jump the fence on the diagonal. Proceed straight forward and turn left into the track. Either go all round the school, past your original starting point again and then turn left over the third jump, or jump the third jump in the opposite direction immediately after your turn—if the horse is sufficiently balanced.

You will easily see that there is quite a variety of patterns you can ride which include the fences on the diagonals and the trotting poles and fence on the centre line. Jump the fences on the diagonals from either direction, but do not attempt to jump the fence with trotting poles backwards as this will only confuse and upset the horse.

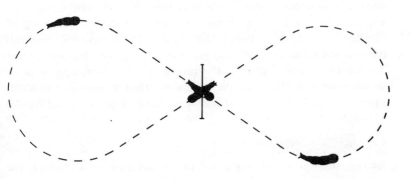

Diagram B: School set up with one fence (a low spread which can be jumped both ways) on the centre to teach the horse to judge correct take-off zone

These exercises can be started at trot, and later performed at canter, too. When jumping from a canter, remember that you must alter the distances between the cavaletti in front of the fence on the centre line. As trotting poles they should be from 4½ feet to 5½ feet apart depending on your horse's stride (4½ feet is the normal). For cantering through so that the horse takes no stride but simply bounces between each cavaletti, they should be 12 feet apart and on their highest position, i.e. from 12″ to 20″ high. There should be about 24 feet between the last cavaletti and the fence. The horse will then bounce between each cavaletti and take one stride in canter before the fence.

Another way of setting up the arena which is very useful when you want to do some jumping exercises to improve your horse's ability to judge his own correct take-off zone, is to set up one small spread fence, which can be jumped from either side, right in the centre of the school on the line B–E (see diagram B). Then proceed to ride a figure of eight, jumping this fence slightly on the slant as you come across the diagonal from any direction.

This jumping on an angle is a very good way to teach a horse to judge the correct take-off spot and is particularly useful for horses who find timing difficult when you start jumping in canter. Jumping from the trot the horse doesn't have to learn much about timing as he can take off at any moment due to the fact that he will always have one pair of feet on the ground. In canter, however, he must be much more accurate and he has to learn how to judge the height of a fence and how to position himself for the take off. When you start this exercise of jumping across the fence, do not make your angle of approach too acute, but keep fairly close to the centre line. Gradually, as the horse becomes accustomed to the exercise, you can increase the angle at which you jump. But remember, the horse must ALWAYS be going straight to jump well—that means he must be straight in himself, with the quarters directly behind the head, running straight through the corridor of the rider's legs and hands.

Care needed setting courses

At this stage it is important not to set too difficult a problem for your horse. You keep the fences small, even though they should be varied and some should be spread and some upright. The sort of problem which might be too much for the young jumper would be jumping immediately after a sharp turn, or positioning jumps in such a way that the horse cannot easily approach them straight and balanced.

Designing a course for a green horse take care to make it flowing, offering no acute angles and no places where a rider would have to check back too hard, or turn too sharply to get to a fence. I am sure that if you give the subject a little thought you will be able to come up with many suitable courses, but I would like to offer three basic designs to start you thinking.

In diagram (C) we have a simple course which could be jumped equally well in the opposite direction, when jump number 3 would become number 2 and jump number 2 would become number 3 but the others would remain the same. The course starts out over a simple brush fence, perhaps with a rail 3″ or so over the top. Keep the first fence small, perhaps only about 2 feet or 2 feet six inches to start with. You will probably want to jump the whole course in trot the first time and if the jumps are very small you will not feel the need to 'drive' your horse too much into the fences and upset his rhythm or cause him to canter. If he does canter the last stride or two into the fence do not attempt to bring him back to trot until the landing side of the jump. At two strides you are much too close to the jump to interfere and must leave the horse alone, until he has landed.

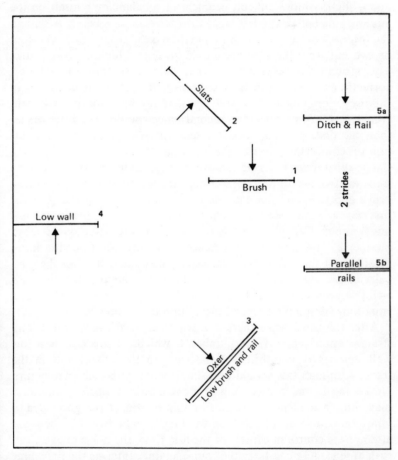

Diagram C: A simple course which can also be started in the opposite direction, when jump 3 would become jump 2, and jump 2 would become 3, but the others would remain the same. The combination is set up to allow two strides (30ft to 36ft)

The first fence is set about two-thirds of the way down the long side of the arena—if you are jumping inside—allowing plenty of room for a balanced approach after a wide curve to the right. After landing you have a long straight line on which to bring the horse back to trot, if you wish, or to steady and balance his canter before the next corner which is again a wide right handed curve.

The second fence, which, in the diagram, is flat wooden boards called slats, is set approximately on the diagonal about two-thirds of the way across. This presents the horse with a very easy approach and a slightly more difficult problem of rebalancing himself on the landing side before the left hand turn to fence number 3. Although the second fence is an upright it should have a ground line set a foot or two out from the base, as should all fences for the green horse. This ground line plays a big part in helping the horse to take off correctly and make a good bascule over his fences. If he jumps in this way, jumping is easy and pleasant for him and he will gain confidence very rapidly. The second fence should be a little higher than the first, probably about 3 feet but still small enough to be jumped comfortably in trot the first time or two around.

The third fence is set on the other diagonal in approximately the same relative position as the second. This is a small oxer made up of brush and rails and presents the horse with a little spread. For the first time around keep the height to about 3 feet and the spread not much more. The problems here are much the same as at fence number 2. The approach is perfectly straightforward but the horse must be re-balanced on landing, before the corner. It is not the difficulty of the individual fences here which is of importance, but how well you keep your horse balanced and calm in a potentially exciting situation, i.e. jumping several fences in quick succession.

After the third fence there is a wide easy right turn and a long straight approach to fence number 4, which, in this case is a low wall, set nearly two-thirds of the way up the school and in the track. Although this should be a simple fence with such an easy turn preceeding it and a nice long approach, this is where your horse may show a tendency to rush. For this reason, it is a good idea to jump the course in trot, at least the first time or two. If, when you attempt the course in canter for the first time, the horse does indeed rush at fence number 4, try the course again, cantering the first three fences, then coming back to trot for the corner and the whole approach to fence number 4, and then, if all goes well, cantering on round the final right curve and jumping the final in-and-out in canter.

The fifth jump is an in-and-out and consists of two fences with 36 feet between them to allow the horse room for two canter strides. The first element is a "ditch and rails" the ditch being simulated by a blanket or sacking laid on the ground in front of the fence, or draped over the low rail. I like to use such unusual additions to courses, even for very green horses, as it helps to prevent horses, or riders, from being spooked by some unusual element in a course during competition later on. Some horses will pay no attention at all to a blanket draped over a fence, and others will certainly notice it, look at it and even shy from it, so keep the jump itself very low to ensure getting the horse over the first time with no problems. After two strides the second element of the fifth fence is a small parallel rails. At this stage of training I do not recommend making the rails truly parallel. I usually keep the front rail three or four inches lower than the back rail, to make quite sure that the horses can see the entire fence clearly. Actually, if the spread is less than four feet the horse jumps the obstacle exactly as he would jump an upright fence and the rider should do the same thing. Do not think "Oh, goodness, there's a spread on this jump, I must ride it extra hard". This will only result in upsetting or hurrying your horse. You should approach all fences with quiet determination in an actively forward moving gait, whether it is trot or canter. Your seat should be on the horse during the approach keeping him straight, with his quarters directly behind his head, your hands should be low, steady and following and should yield the rein to the horse over the fence.

Jumping a combination may prove a little more exciting to your horse and he may try to rush off after the last jump. Do not permit this. You must bring him quietly back to a walk, preferably on a straight line after the last fence, before turning the corner. If you have real difficulty doing this you can circle the horse to the left in the corner of the school immediately following the fence. If you do this two or three times the horse will expect to be turned left, into the wall, and will prepare himself automatically for this by slowing down immediately after the jump. If the young horse is properly prepared for jumping his first course and is ridden calmly and with confidence, this measure should not be necessary, but it is a useful little trick to use with rushers you may have to retrain or horses which have been wrongly started.

On the day you first decide to jump your young horse round his first course, work him on the flat first for at least twenty minutes to half an hour. Make sure he is balanced, supple and attentive before you even think about jumping. Then start some work on the flat in amongst your jumps and then trot him over the brush fence three or four times in each direction. You will probably want to jump each fence individually before attempting the whole course. Approach each one calmly and quietly and bring the horse to a walk as soon as possible after each fence, without being rough.

Then attempt the whole course, perhaps starting out in trot and cantering fences four and five (a) and (b). If the horse is calm and unhurried, try the whole course in a balanced canter. If he gets excited half way through, stop and work a little more on the flat before continuing the course. If all goes well, twice round the course

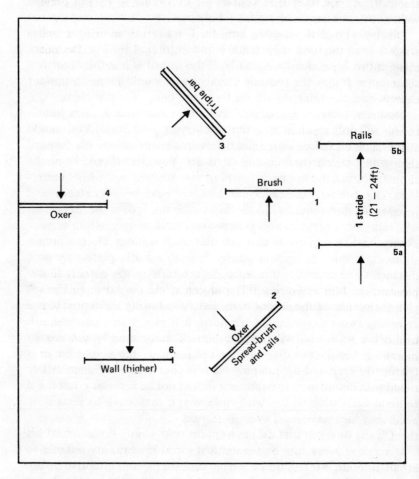

Diagram D: A harder course, incorporating a one stride in-and-out and with fence 6 a little higher (say 3ft 6ins to 3ft 9ins). Note that fence 6 is placed well down the school allowing plenty of time for a straight approach.

is plenty for one lesson, especially after jumping most of the fences two or three times beforehand as suggested. If you do not feel that your second go round was sufficiently smooth and good to finish on, take the first three fences again, quietly in canter; the constant changes of direction will ensure that the horse remains calm and attentive and you should get three really good fences to finish on a positive note. If so, stop there, cool the horse out, give him a carrot, a pat and a word of appreciation and return him to his stable. It is important that your horse knows when he has done well, not only when he has NOT pleased you.

Diagram (D) shows a more difficult course, incorporating a one stride in-and-out and with fence 6 higher (say 3 ft. 6″). Do not attempt this type of course until your horse has had about four to six months of jumping training and is working well on the flat and calmly over easy courses.

The course shown in diagram (D) is still very flowing with wide turns and good approaches to all the fences, but now we have a one stride in-and-out which requires more confidence from the horse than a two stride combination. It is also essential that the horse should be straight over both fences or the distance will become too long. The normal distance for one stride for a trained horse in show jumping is 26 ft., but with the fences very low and a green horse who will certainly be travelling in a slow, shortened canter, 21 ft. to 24 ft. is usually a better distance. A big horse will find 21 ft. a little short and a smaller horse may find 24 ft. slightly long, so adjust your distance very carefully to your horse to make things as easy and pleasant for him as you can. The object of jumping training is to give the horse confidence in you, his rider. He must learn to trust you completely and jump anything you face him at. This confidence cannot come overnight but must be carefully nurtured by you over months of training. You must never allow the horse to hurt or frighten himself when jumping, which means that you must never overface him and you must always investigate any jumps you plan to use outside to be absolutely certain that they are safe and have a good landing and a good take off, before presenting your horse at them.

Diagram (E) shows a longer, more difficult course, which incorporates two treble combinations. This is the type of course you should be using after about eight months to one year of jumping training. The approaches to the fences are still from wide easy turns, there are no surprises of fences straight out of the corner, or difficult turns to be made. Fence number 1 should be kept low and simple. Fence number 2 consists of three elements, a spread, not too big, maybe 3 ft. 3″ high and about 4 ft. wide to start with, followed by two strides,

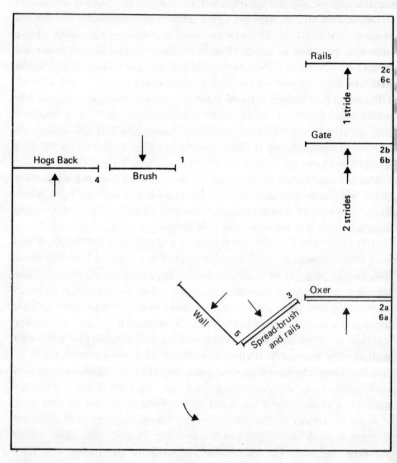

Diagram E: A longer, more difficult course, incorporating combinations. Make fence 5 a higher fence (perhaps 3ft 6ins in the first round but 3ft 9ins to 4ft on your second round).

approximately 36 ft., and an upright fence of about 3 ft. 3″ followed by one stride and another upright fence. The distance required between two upright fences is slightly more than the distance between two spread fences and 26 ft. will probably be the most comfortable distance for your horse when going on in a rather stronger canter than you would use for a beginner course.

After the final element of fence number 2 take care to bring your horse back to you before the corner and make a good turn to the third fence. It is as well to remember that most horses try to fall in, particularly on left hand turns, due to stiffness and an unwillingness to bend around the corners. This poor negotiation of the corner prior to the fence is the major cause for faults at the fence. Take time and patience to bring your horse round each corner balanced and correctly bent. The secret is to check him and shorten the stride immediately upon landing and before arriving at the corner. Then use the outside leg and hand to turn the horse and not the inside hand. If you use the inside rein to turn your horse, you will lose control of the hindquarters, which are your engine. The hindquarters will swing out to the right and the horse will not be running straight between your legs and hands. Certainly, the inside leg has a part to play in turning the horse, but think of turning him much more with your outside leg and hand and you will stand a much better chance of bringing the forehand around the quarters and keeping the horse straight and balanced.

After the third fence, which should be spread a little, maybe about four feet in width, again bring your horse back to you and rebalance him before the corner. The fourth fence is comparatively simple, with a good approach, but again be careful to ride THROUGH the corner following the fence. Now is a good time to introduce a slightly higher fence and number 5 could, perhaps, be a wall at around 3 ft. 9 ins. to 4 ft. in height. Start out the first time around with the wall at 3 ft. 6 ins. and then raise it for your second round.

After the wall, again sit down and bring your horse back to you before the corner and approach the treble in-and-out again balanced and straight and with lots of determination.

It is also possible to change this course and make it a lot more demanding by making the treble in-and-out jumpable from either direction and taking it immediately after fence number 4 as the fifth fence and then making a right turn and finishing over the wall as fence number 6. Do not try this kind of course until your horse is really confident and fluent in his jumping. The first big difficulty is that the combination fence would necessarily be quite close to the corner of your arena and you will have only a short approach. This demands that you ride the two preceding corners with tremendous accuracy and balance. The wall, which would then become your sixth fence, will also be more difficult jumped in the opposite direction because the approach will be considerably shorter. However, jumped in this way the course would become quite testing and interesting for a more experienced horse.

Jumping combinations

Provided you keep the fences small, it is a good plan to introduce doubles and trebles into your courses fairly early on. The length of the canter stride will vary from horse to horse, but at this stage of training it is as well to stick to a distance of either 36 ft. or 24 ft. which will be either two, or one non-jumping stride. If the horse is

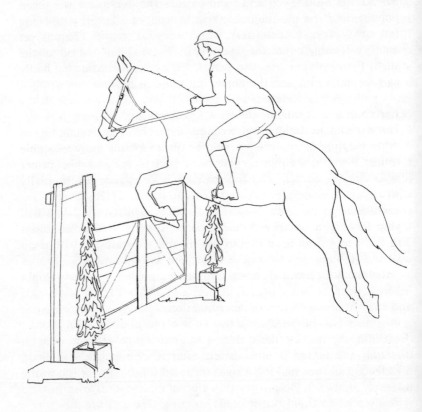

Jumping with confidence

very green and therefore going on a very shortened stride, reduce these distances 3 feet or so.

It is particularly important to approach combinations straight and balanced. If you are right at the first fence you will be right all the way through. Make sure your horse jumps straight over the centre of each fence. Ensure this by sitting down and driving between each fence, and looking up over the centre of the last fence all the way down the line.

Throughout all your jumping training, remember that jumping in a confined space, i.e. an indoor school, is much more difficult for the horse than jumping outside in a nice big field or show ring. The room for error is reduced drastically when the size of the arena makes only a few strides possible between each fence. The horse MUST be absolutely straight and balanced round his corners when jumping a tight course indoors, though he might get away with being far less balanced if the same course were set outside. This is yet another reason for keeping your fences very small indeed at the start of your jumping training and increasing their size only gradually as your horse gains in confidence and suppleness.

Early warning signals that things are going wrong
Horses don't just suddenly go wrong and start refusing or running out or developing other problems. For the observant and knowledgeable trainer there are a dozen early warning signals. The sensitive trainer will take immediate action and put things right before they go really wrong.

One of the first signs that all is not well and that the horse will stop sooner or later, is that the horse will put in a short stride just in front of the jump, instead of jumping it properly, with a good parabola, in his stride. Another such signal is that the horse does not jump straight across the centre of the fence and continue straight forward, but twists to the left or right just before take off and jumps one side of the fence, and then turns sharply in that direction after the jump. This evasion is often used by a scared horse.

If the horse is rushing, there is a moment just after landing when you let him sprawl, for just one stride, but then you pick him up and re-balance him. Always check before the corner following fences. Never allow a horse to rush round corners unbalanced and then try to check in front of the next fence.

If the horse is rushing really badly and snatching the bit and taking off three strides from the fence, it is because he is frightened. Don't give him anything to grab, check him and drop the bit and check again immediately, but don't allow yourself to pull constantly. You have to be very quick and light with the hand. The important thing is to sit properly, deep in the saddle, on your seat bones, without hollowing your back or leaning forward, so that you create for yourself a firm platform from which to work.

16 *When Things go Wrong*

Sometimes, during jumping training, things may not go according to plan. The horse may start approaching his jumps nervously, refusing, running out, propping at the take-off, bucking over his fences, bucking or kicking after jumping, rushing into his fences with his head in the air, and getting over excited.

Causes of jumping problems: first diagnose the cause of trouble

These jumping problems may be due to one of a variety of reasons. First of all, it may be simply lack of sufficient training—or overfacing, the horse being asked to jump fences which are too big or difficult for the stage he is at. Or the horse may have previously suffered a fall and consequently have lost his nerve. He may be weak and lack sufficient condition to jump comfortably. Or he may be suffering pain, perhaps pain from the saddle or bridle which may be wrongly fitted. He may simply have the memory of pain from being hit in the mouth when jumping.

Refusing
This horse is being overfaced.

More likely, the rider may be at fault, shortening the stride too much on the approach, interfering with the horse as he tries to jump, presenting him badly, not turning the corner before the fence correctly; or the rider may be simply lacking in determination or ability. Riders very often lean or fall forwards on the approach to a fence and consequently drop the horse into the bottom of it, never giving him a chance to jump. Or the rider may be looking down at the fence on the approach, instead of looking straight ahead over the centre of it. Looking down on the part of the rider can be sufficient in itself to stop a young horse. It has the effect of hunching the rider's shoulders and pulling his seat forward out of the saddle, thus removing his main driving aid. Or the rider may be clinging with his lower leg instead of keeping it free so that he can use it on the approach if necessary.

The first step to curing any fault in the horse's way of going is to diagnose the cause of the trouble correctly. After that you use your common sense to correct it. If the problem is lack of training, go back to working the horse over low, varied fences in the loose jumping ring, and then on the lunge. It is much better to keep the fences very small during the horse's first year of jumping than to have him start refusing due to overfacing. Very often, it is the rider who stops the horse because he is nervous of the larger fence. In this case, lower the fence, to the ground if necessary, and get the horse going freely.

Set up situations to work for you

It is a very good idea to let a young horse follow the lead of an older, more experienced horse when starting jumping. Allow the young horse to come along about five or six yards behind the schoolmaster and he will very quickly gain confidence. After jumping the fence behind the experienced horse a couple of times, have the young horse go on over it alone next time.

As in all your training, with jumping particularly, it is important to set everything up so that nothing can possibly go wrong, everything is working in your favour. For instance, if you know the horse to be sticky at a particular obstacle, jump it towards home instead of away from home, and have a lead horse with you in case of difficulties.

Never attempt to jump at all until you have the horse moving freely and calmly forward between your hand and leg, and take great care that fences are placed so that it is easy for the horse to get to them straight, and balanced. Don't, for instance, jump just coming out of a corner, which would be much too difficult for your horse at this stage.

If your problems are being caused by any obvious rider faults— for example, the rider over-shortening the stride during the approach, bad presentation, lack of determination, or rider hanging on by the reins or clinging with the lower leg—you must put somebody else on the horse, because that rider is not capable of teaching the horse anything at that stage.

Stable management problems

If your problems are due to the horse's weakness, soreness, or badly fitting or uncomfortable tack, these are matters of stable management. If the horse is weak despite apparently correct feeding, have the vet check his teeth, which may be sharp. If it is some time since they were floated (rasped) they could make it so painful for him to chew his food that he simply may not be getting the benefit of whatever you are feeding him. He should also be checked for worms, which can pull a horse down badly if he is not dosed regularly, at least four times a year.

In the case of soreness or tenderness in a leg or foot, do not attempt to jump the horse again until your veterinarian is quite certain that any splint, or tendon problems are cleared up. Young horses are especially susceptible to splints, and jumping, even over very small fences, subjects the legs to a great deal of strain and concussion. If there is no visible sign of leg trouble, have the horse-shoer check your horse's feet for corns or bruised soles.

Badly fitting tack, which is uncomfortable for the horse, can take his mind so much off what you are asking him to do that it could be a cause of his starting to refuse fences. Make sure that your bit fits your horse and that it is correctly adjusted. A bit which is too wide will slide back and forth in the horse's mouth and bruise him. A bit which is too narrow will pinch his mouth. A bit fitted too low will annoy him by banging against the backs of his teeth. Incidentally, it is also an open invitation to him to start putting his tongue over the bit. A bit that is too high and is pulling his lips into a fiersome grin, may also be sufficiently unpleasant for the horse to take his attention away from his rider. The snaffle should rest comfortably in the corners of the mouth, making about one and a half folds in the corners of the mouth. Make sure that your martingale fits properly. You do not want to have a constant downward pull on the reins by the rings of a running martingale. It should be adjusted so that it does not act at all when the horse has his head in the correct normal position, but only comes into operation when the head is raised above the angle of control. And be sure to use rein stops with a running martingale, to avoid the rings being caught on the ends of the reins at the bit.

Your saddle should fit your horse correctly. See that it is properly stuffed and doesn't pinch his withers or press on his spine. If you use a saddle pad, draw it well into the channel of the saddle as you girth up, so that no pressure is transmitted to the spine via the pad. Do not ride the horse if he is galled, or has a sore back. Treat the wound and wait for it to heal before resuming your schooling.

Horses who rush their fences

A keen young horse may easily develop the habit of rushing his fences. Rushing is nearly always due to fear—often fear of the rider's hands. The rider may be catching the horse in the mouth over the fence, or he may be taking a pull or a tighter hold on the horse's head in front of the fence. In any case, rushing is cured on the landing side of the fence, and not on the take off side, and the rider must learn to leave the horse's head alone and try not to upset him when approaching a fence. Pulling at him will only cause him to raise his head higher and fight, and he will rush his fences even more.

There are several ways to deal with this problem. First of all, try working on a circle instead of on a straight line. Work on the circle tends to reduce natural impulsion, whereas working on a straight line tends to increase it. Keep the fences very low, and go back to jumping from the trot. Work the horse round the circle, passing close to the jump, and when he is going freely and calmly forward, increase the circle to include the jump and then reduce the circle again and miss the jump two or three times. With the jump very low this exercise can be continued for a fairly long period without any harmful effects. The horse should be worked in both directions and as soon as he performs quietly in trot, do the same exercise in canter.

I would emphasise that nearly all rushing is caused in some way or another by the rider. Horses are very sensitive to even the smallest movement of the rider and without even realising it, the rider may be causing the horse to rush by something as slight as an increased hold with the thigh, or an almost imperceptible shortening of the reins. He may even be causing the horse to rush by being excited or

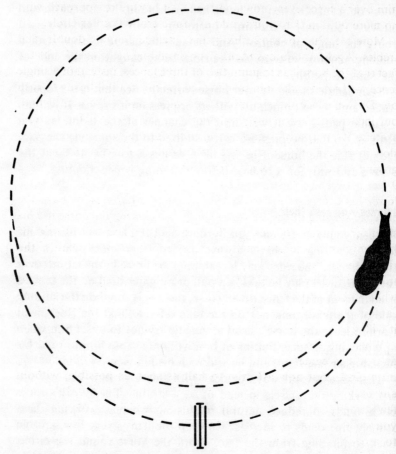

Exercise round the circle for a rushing horse

apprehensive in his THOUGHTS about the jump. This is not an exaggeration. Ultimately, we aim to train the horse to respond to such light aids that many sensitive thoroughbreds become mind readers. So, compose yourself and think calmly about the job in hand.

Some horses get over-excited whenever they see a course of jumps. This will rarely be the case with a young horse you are training from scratch, but is quite a frequent problem with horses brought in for re-schooling. In this case, it is a good idea to do your work on the flat in amongst a course of fences for several days. When the horse settles, probably after a day or two, by all means jump him over a fence every now and then, but be sure to approach with no more tension than you would ask for a trot or canter circle.

More exercises for the rushing horse include jumping doubles and trebles. Again, the jumps themselves should be quite small, but the fact that the horse has to jump two or three fences, instead of a single fence, will often make him take a good look instead of trying to rush on. Do not place these combinations along a straight line at first, but incorporate them into your work on the circle. If the trotting exercise over a single fence on a circle is not working, or seems slow in getting any result, place trotting poles, 4½ feet apart, on the ground in front of the fence. Three poles will be sufficient, and leave 9 feet between the last pole and the fence. This will make the horse lower his head and look where he is going and will also have the effect of slowing down the trot slightly and making the horse use his shoulder muscles to pick his feet up higher. The trot should be kept rhythmic going through the poles and it is usually best if the rider rises to the trot. The poles must be removed before attempting to canter the fence, but if the very first pole is left on the ground when the other two are removed, the horse will have exactly one canter stride after crossing the pole before jumping the fence, and it will act as a 'take off' cavaletti.

When the horse has gained enough confidence to jump calmly at trot and canter on the circle, continue the exercise of jumping on a circle, but now ask him to halt as soon as possible, without any roughness, on the landing side of the jump. It may take quite a few strides at first, but very quickly the horse will get the idea that you are going to stop him after the fence, and you will be able to come to a calm, balanced halt in three or four strides. Remember that the reins are NOT the brakes. The brake is in your seat. You must sit down and create a strong platform on the horse with your seat and thigh. Then you simply ride him forward with your seat and resist with your hand—ceasing to allow him to go forward. At no time should you raise your hands and pull and yank at the horse's mouth.

From here your progress should be rapid. As soon as the horse stops without a fight after jumping the single fence, start riding him round small courses which include many changes of direction. Start out in trot and make a halt after each fence. Provided he works quietly, continue with the exercise in canter. If he is really going calmly, don't stop after each fence, but make one or perhaps two halts during the course, always ensuring that the horse comes to a halt on a straight line as soon as possible after landing over the fence.

Be particularly careful how you ride round the corners of your jumping course. No horse should have the slightest difficulty actually jumping the small fences you will be using at this stage. The lesson, therefore, is not concerned with "getting the horse over the jump" but rather with getting the horse from one jump to another in a balanced fashion so that he can jump the fences correctly in stride and make a good bascule over each jump, using his head and neck and back correctly. Never allow him to whisk around a corner so that you lose control of his quarters and he falls along on his forehand to the next jump. Make certain that he canters calmly and smoothly around reasonable curves at each change of direction, and be careful to set your courses so that they allow the young horse plenty of room to perform correctly.

Running out

Running out, that is, refusing to jump the fence by running past it on one side or the other, is always a "rider" fault. It is the result of the rider failing to keep the horse moving straight through his legs and hands with the quarters directly behind the head. It nearly always happens because the rider has failed to ride the previous corner correctly and has therefore not been able to present the horse at the fence moving straight.

If your horse does ever run out, stop him as soon as you possibly can—preferably level with the fence, and turn him back towards the fence before re-presenting him. For example if he ran out left, leaving the fence on your right. Turn him to the right, send him back along the approach line, fast, stop him again and then turn and represent him to the fence, making certain this time that he is absolutely straight.

I do not advocate punishing a young horse with a whip. It is true that it may occasionally be necessary, but in my experience nearly all faults that horses make when jumping are entirely due to bad riding, or at least, slowness of reaction of the rider, and punishing the horse for faults of the rider makes no sense. Certainly no rider, unless very experienced, should attempt to take his hand off the rein and hit his horse just before take off. This nearly always results in startling and unbalancing the horse and causing him either to refuse or to hit the fence.

17

Whips, Spurs, and Martingales

Objects of schooling

It pays to bear in mind all the time your objectives in schooling your horse. The first objective is to keep him calm, the second is to confirm him in what he knows so far, and the third, into which the second objective merges, is to continue the horse's progressive education.

If you fail to keep the horse calm, you will necessarily fail in all your objectives. In previous chapters I have already stressed the importance of starting out each day's work with a period of warming up and loosening up, mainly in free walk on a long rein. When the horse has had a chance to move around for five or ten minutes, you can pick up the rein and work with more energy in trot and walk. This method of starting work each day will ensure that you keep the horse calm and will allow you to achieve your second and third objectives.

After an initial fifteen minutes or so, I work my horse for perhaps half an hour doing basic work, mostly in trot, unless the lesson for that day is to be in canter, in which case I will do more preliminary work in canter. At this point I am not very demanding of the horse, but keep him well within his limits, and thus cool and calm. After this part of the lesson I let the horse rest with a few minutes walking on a loose rein. Then the lesson continues, repeating much of the same basic work, but this time demanding more from the horse, until he is working up to the best standard he is capable of achieving. During this part of the lesson I will ask much more energy and impulsion from the horse, for certain movements, but it is important to remember to keep these demands very brief and to give him frequent rest periods between demands. One of my favourite quotations is from a Frenchman, Captain Beudant, who said 'Ask often, be content with little, and reward very much.'

This quotation should be put into practice particularly for the final part of the lesson, which should follow after another rest at the relaxed walk. The new work which the horse has not yet mastered should be tried now, just for five or ten minutes. Ask for just one or two steps of the movement you are teaching, then allow the horse to relax, which is really a reward, then ask again and so on. Practice the new work four or five times and then take the horse back to the stable. The cessation of work in itself is perhaps the most easily understood reward for the horse. He will soon learn that if he tries hard when you ask him some new or more difficult questions, that very quickly you will reward him with the pleasure and complete rest of his grooming, feed and comfortable loose box.

Developing the muscles

I stress this point of asking for new and therefore more difficult movements for only a few moments at a time at first because it is important to keep in mind that unaccustomed work will very quickly cause the horse to feel stiffness in his muscles. If it is continued beyond a very brief period, before the horse has developed the necessary muscular ability, it will cause stiffness and pain which may last for days. It is easy to overlook this point because the rider doesn't always realise just what an effort he is asking the horse to make when bringing untrained muscles into play.

The idea behind training on the flat is to develop suppleness in every muscle and joint of the horse, so we must take care not to overdo things at first and produce stiffness. Stiffness anywhere, either in horse or rider, leads to stiffness everywhere, and stiffness in any part of the horse will certainly show up as resistance to the bit. Remain alert and observant and the horse will give you plenty of indication of whether you are going too far and causing him dis-comfort or pain.

Reward often

The question of just how to reward a horse perplexes many riders, but really it is very simple. The horse appreciates a calm, confident, sensible rider. This rider will reward the horse promptly for his efforts by ceasing the movement and allowing the horse to rest for a few moments. This method of rewarding the horse should be part of your everyday riding, whether it is work in the manege or over fences. Certainly you may also give him a pat and speak to him now and then.

If you follow the pattern of a lesson laid out above for your horse and ask for new and more demanding exercises at the end of your work period, you not only give the horse every opportunity to perform them well, by thoroughly suppling and working him first, but you also give him the best possible reward at the end of the session, that of finishing work immediately after he has made his greatest efforts on your behalf.

I do not believe in "punishing" horses, since I am certain that it never does the slightest good but only upsets the horse and destroys our very first objective in schooling, that of keeping the horse calm. The only reason we are able to train horses is that we are mentally far superior to them and we are able to control their great physical strength with our mental superiority. Resorting to violence and punishment belies this mental superiority. Certainly, any horse is capable of being a little naughty at times, or of developing one particular trick or sham. This must be corrected with patience and firmness immediately, and a touch with the whip or the spur is usually quite sufficient in these cases to bring the horse back to order. Every well trained horse should respect his rider, but if he is to perform his work really well, and joyfully, it is important that he should not fear the rider, nor the whip, nor the spur.

Use and abuse of the whip

The whip is a most valuable aid to the trainer and rideı. In the chapters on loose schooling and lungeing I have stressed that the horse should respect, but not fear the whip. This remains true for the ridden horse, and I never ride without carrying a whip, though I use it very seldom.

The horse understands the action of the whip very easily—more easily than he understands the action of the leg, for example—and so the whip, which he can see, as well as feel, if used sensibly, can be a great help in teaching the horse about the actions of the rider's legs.

Later on in the horse's training, the whip is used to reinforce the action of the leg. I prefer to use the whip to the spur in many instances. For example, in teaching a horse to move away from the rider's leg in a half-pass, it makes more sense to use the whip, which can touch the horse on the outside hind leg and indicate to him that he should move that leg away under his body, than to use the spur, which can only touch the horse just behind the girth and its action there may not be fully understood by the horse.

The whip should be used sparingly, but it is very useful in keeping a horse attentive to the leg. If the horse is slow to respond to the action of the leg, his response can be improved by using the whip immediately after and just behind the leg, to support the leg. The

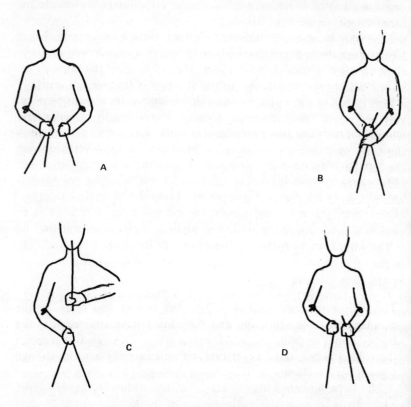

Changing the whip from the right to left

whip should be applied just sharply enough so that the horse knows it has been used, and should not be repeated meaninglessly—once is usually quite enough.

You should practise carrying and using the whip in both the right and the left hand. I frequently come across riders who say that they cannot even carry a whip in the left hand, and this is depriving themselves of a very useful aid, simply through lack of taking the trouble to develop the necessary manual dexterity. When carrying the whip in the hand it should lie across the rider's knee, passing across the palm of the hand and being held in place by the side of the thumb. Held this way the whip will not interfere with the correct position of the rider's hands, nor will it accidentally hit the horse.

When you wish to apply the whip, both reins should be put into one hand and the whip held in the other. Spin the whip around the index finger (rather like a drum Majorette with her baton) and then use the whip once, calmly, and return it to its original position in your hand. When changing a short whip from one hand to the other it is all right to draw it forward with the new hand, rather like drawing a sword, and pass it across in front of the body, but if you are using a long dressage whip you will find that method of changing hands very awkward. Try this method, instead. If you wish to change the whip from the right hand into the left hand; first put both reins and the whip into the right hand, leaving the left hand free. Then pass the left hand in front of the body, raising the elbow slightly and twisting the wrist so that when the hand grasps the whip the thumb will be round the forward part of the whip and the fingers to the back. Now raise the end of the whip so that it passes in front of your face in an upright position (*see illustration*).

The whip is always used in a free hand—that is, with the reins held in the other hand—to avoid jerking on the mouth at the same time as applying the whip.

If your horse is frightened of the whip, due to past bad handling or misuse of the whip, teach him gradually not to fear it. The best way to do this is to carry the whip all the time, although this may be hard at first. If you never carry it he will never become sufficiently accustomed to it to get over his fear. All fear of the whip is due to past misuse of the whip, since the unhandled horse has no past experience of pain from the whip and no reason to fear what appears to him a simple stick.

Use and misuse of the spur

The spur is really essential once you get beyond the elementary stages of training. With the spur the rider can get refined results from finely shaded actions of the leg. The use of the leg aids, as with all aids, is progressive, starting with the seat bone, pressure of the thigh or knee, a light squeeze with the top of the calf, followed by a graduated use of the lower leg, the inside of the heel, and culminating in a touch of the spur. If you are not wearing spurs, then the final resort left to you is the heel of the boot, which cannot possibly give you the precision or refinement of the spur used exactly on the correct spot at exactly the right moment. Worse still, the use of the heel is likely to develop into kicking, which should be reserved for footballs and not used on horses.

Provided the rider is able to sit correctly, with the lower leg still, there is no reason to ride without spurs. Of course, if the rider is still at the stage where he cannot control his lower leg and he is likely to jam his spur into the horse unwittingly, he should not wear them. The spurs that I use are simply dummies, and I do not believe that rowelled spurs are ever necessary, except, perhaps, with a very advanced rider on a very advanced horse which requires the most refined and precise application of the aids, and that comes beyond the scope of this book.

The horse has to be taught about the meaning of the spur, just as he has to be taught the meaning of the leg. In your early training you carry a whip, but you do not wear spurs. You use the whip if necessary to reinforce the aid given by the leg. The spur must always be used very sparingly, and very precisely. It should be used just behind the girth in a forward movement and not jabbed into the horse with the rider's toe pointed down. It is often applied too far back on the horse's flank, and this is what causes a horse to kick at the spur.

The spur is never dug into the horse and kept there. It should be used to brush against the coat lightly, or if necessary to give a very light pinch against the horse, in which case it must be an instantaneous action and never held in place. The action may be repeated, lightly, several times, but it should be as quick and light as possible.

Some old books talk about the "lesson of the spur" and by this they mean that the horse is submitted to a prolonged "attack" with the spurs, driving him forwards, but at the same time he is held forcibly in place with the reins. This "lesson" is supposed to force the horse into a state of submission to the rider. Fortunately, these methods are no longer used today, although you do still see grave misuse of the spur, usually brought about by the rider losing his temper—a state of affairs which should never happen at all. No one can master a horse until he can first master himself. This "lesson of the spur" seems to have obtained very doubtful results, in any case. Auber, speaking of Baucher's horses who were subjected to this attack, says:– "they worked with clockwork regularity, but in a state of deadly sadness".

Martingales

It is my belief that most horses should be schooled without the help of a martingale. However, if the horse has a very long neck and a long back and a naturally very high head carriage I see nothing wrong in using a martingale, correctly fitted, to assist the rider in developing the correct carriage in the horse. Certainly an experienced rider can overcome these problems without resorting to a martingale,

Standing martingale

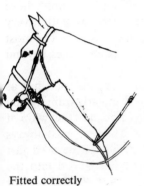

Fitted correctly   Fitted incorrectly

but it will take him longer than if he used one, and provided always that the martingale is correctly fitted, I do not believe that it does any harm.

The purpose of the martingale is NOT to hold the horse's head down. It is to prevent it from rising above the angle of control. There is a great difference. I do not use a standing martingale in training at all, except perhaps when taking a very high headed horse out hunting, when a standing martingale may prevent him from throwing his head right up and hitting me on the face with his neck. I recommend the use of the running martingale in training, if one is needed at all.

Most people who object to the running martingale, do so because it acts on the bit, but I would point out that it doesn't act at all if the horse's head is in the correct place, and it doesn't act at all unless the rider also uses the reins. That is, with the rein loose, there is no martingale, therefore, the rider has complete control of the amount of pressure brought to bear by the martingale and the horse cannot learn to lean against it as he certainly can with a standing martingale.

The running martingale should be fitted so that, with the rider mounted, and the horse standing correctly to attention, on a contact, there is absolutely no downward pull on the reins. If there is, the martingale is too short. It should only act when the horse raises his head above the angle of control. Then the rider can bring the head down easily and quickly by the action of his legs and hands, and the horse cannot escape that action by raising his head still more and letting the bit slip into the corners of his mouth.

Running martingale

Fitted correctly   Fitted incorrectly

Using a martingale does have one other good point, too. There is always a neckstrap round the horse's neck for the rider to slip a finger into to avoid hitting a young horse in the mouth.

Never, under any circumstances, would I advocate the use of running reins, or the so-called "German martingale". I have schooled and re-schooled many hundreds of horses and I have never found this device necessary. It has the awful effect of bending the horse's neck at the third or fourth vertebra instead of at the poll, and this is encouraging the horse to use an evasion to the rider's aids which is extremely difficult to cure. When the horse tucks his head down too low with his chin on his chest, he is totally out of control and if this ever happens he must be immediately driven up with the legs and put back into the proper shape, or the evasion will become a habit.

Whatever artificial aids you decide to use in your training, always remember that it is not WHAT you use, but HOW you use it that matters. Keep your three objectives of schooling in mind at all times, and particularly the first objective, that of keeping the horse calm.

18

Hunting Your Four Year Old

If your young horse is well developed, as he should be after several months of training on the lines laid down in earlier chapters, it is a good plan to take him out for some very short days hunting at this stage. Always remember your first objective in schooling—to keep the horse calm—and you will have to be particularly careful about this when you take him out hunting, or to horse shows, where just being amongst a crowd of other horses will tend to excite him considerably.

Take along a companion

Taking your young horse out hunting, or to small horse shows, serves several useful purposes. It introduces him to the necessity of obeying his rider and remaining calm, even amidst exciting circumstances. It provides an often necessary diversion and stimulus— young horses are liable to get bored and sour if ridden continually in an arena at home. It increases the horse's natural impulsion, and it helps enormously in his jumping training, since it develops his desire to go on and jump at the same time as giving him a great deal of experience of negotiating many different obstacles on varying terrain.

It is often a good plan to take along an older horse as schoolmaster on the first few occasions you take your youngster out with hounds. You do not want him to get over-excited and the presence of an older stable companion will do much to keep him calm. On the very first occasion you take him out, stay well away from the crowd. Find a quiet spot where you, and your stable mate, can keep quietly moving about at walk and trot. If your youngster settles well and is prepared to stand still, after fifteen minutes or so, encourage him to do so. But never insist on making him stand still if he is nervous and upset, let him keep quietly on the move. This way you will avoid tempting him to lash out at other horses, or rear, or show his anxiety in any other manner.

Stay away from the crowd

When hounds move off, keep well away to one side and follow from there. Do not get bunched up with a crowd of horses at the back of the hunt—nothing is more liable to make your youngster start pulling than that. If hounds are cantering on to their covert, start cantering, well away from the rest of the field, with a loose rein. No horse can pull, if the rider doesn't first pull at him. Try to ride extra calmly with a very quiet seat and gentle, but firm aids. Simply do not let him pull by never giving him anything to pull against. Keep him moving quietly along beside his stable companion, and if he does get very over-excited, or out of hand, keep him moving on large circles and work your way away from the hunt and take him quietly back home. You will find that after hill-topping for a few weeks most young horses, if they are quietly and sensibly handled, will settle down very well and you can follow on for a little bit longer each time.

Provided your young horse is going along fairly calmly, you may certainly canter along and jump any small fences, similar to those he has been jumping at home, that come your way. On no account, however, allow him to 'race' alongside another horse. This is asking for trouble and would probably end up in an injury to you or the horse. Be sensible about your jumping, too. Don't overface a young horse, and don't wait in an excited throng of horses for your turn to jump a fence, keep him moving about quietly, away from the crowd, or, better still, if there is no wire and it is safe to do so, find your own spot and jump him on his own.

How long to stay out

As the season wears on, keep your youngster out a little longer and jump some fences that are a little bigger. I cannot tell you exact times to keep him out with hounds, but be very conscious of his physical and mental state at all times and never overstress or tire him. Certainly an hour is plenty to start with, and it would be a rare young horse who would not be tired by two hours out with the hunt. If he is a highly strung youngster he may not show his physical tiredness, but if you overstress him you will very quickly bring on a splint or a curb or some other youthful physical ailment, and it certainly isn't worth laying the horse up for weeks just because you asked too much of him too soon.

Let your youngster 'have a go'

If the weather is good and the going is reasonable, once your youngster knows what it's all about, choose a quiet day in late December or early January when the leaves are off the trees and

Taking your youngster out with hounds

hedges, and the grass has died down, and there aren't too many people out because they are doing their Christmas shopping, or recovering from their New Year feasting, and let him canter on freely after the hounds. If possible, jump a few fences in your own place, without a lead and let your horse really try a little. After this you will find that he will gain experience very quickly.

Whenever possible, hack to the meet. This will help him to settle down and will "take the edge off" him before you present him with the sudden excitements of hunting. It will also mean that you have to hack home, and this will give you ample opportunity to cool the horse out thoroughly on the way and avoid any danger of colic through nervous excitement. It will, of course, depend on where you live, whether you can do this or not. You would not want to hack a young horse more than three or four miles to a meet, and you must adjust the length of time you stay with hounds to the time it is going to take you to hack home afterwards. It is the time they spend out of

the stable that has to be considered with all hunters, not the actual
time you spend hunting.

Teaching him to load and travel

If you do not live close enough to any meets to hack there you will
have to go in a hired horse-box or perhaps in your own trailer.
Either way, it pays to teach your horse to load sensibly and quietly.
It really is not difficult to teach a young horse right from the start
to load into any vehicle. I have seen horses loaded into the back
of pick-up trucks, jumping the two and a half to three feet step up
from the ground, with perfect confidence and calmness; and I have
seen horses refuse to be led up a broad, inviting ramp into a luxurious
horse box. It is all in the way you handle things from the start. You
must handle your horse with complete calmness and confidence.
You must KNOW that he is going to load quietly and obediently.

Before asking a young horse to enter a small horse-trailer or
even a horse box, let him have a good look, and smell, at where you
are asking him to go. Make certain that your trailer is tall enough
for your horse. A tall thoroughbred may be perfectly good to load
into a seven foot high trailer, but may refuse point blank to go anywhere near the entrance of a six foot one. He is not stupid, he knows
he will probably bang his head.

Lead the horse quietly up to the ramp and, if you are lucky
enough to have the walk through type of trailer, open the front
so that there is plenty of light, and an inviting opening for the
horse to look through. Horse's eyes are very simple, when compared
to the human eye, and they take a long time to adjust to changes of
light, so always try to have plenty of light inside the trailer. Try not
to pull on the horse's head. Nothing seems to make a horse less
inclined to go forward than someone standing in front of him pulling
at his head. You do want to keep him facing straight into the trailer,
with his head straight in front of him, if at all possible, but be
cunning about it and don't give him an excuse to pull backwards.

If the horse does not follow you straight inside, as many do, you
can try tempting him with some grain, keeping it well in front of his
nose and low to the ground. Or you can load a stable mate first to
encourage the young horse not to be scared of the trailer. Keep
everyone helping you behind the horse's eye. One person does have
to lead the horse, but everyone else should be positioned so that
their very presence behind the horse tends to drive him forward.

If a horse is very reluctant, try attaching two lunge lines to the sides of the trailer and have one person on the end of each. Lead the horse straight up to the ramp, and as far in as he will willingly

Loading a difficult horse using two lunge lines crossed behind the horse

go, but do not pull him. Have the two people holding the lunge lines cross over behind the horse, so that the lines cross over behind the horse, resting on his hind legs just above the hocks. Then you can exert gentle pressure on the horse from behind, without danger of being kicked, and without any necessity to pull at the horse's head. I have never known this method to fail, but there is one escape route for a horse so held in place, and that is to rear. Most horses won't think of rearing unless someone is pulling at their head, but if he does go up, try to keep his head straight towards the entrance of the trailer. If the horse twists to one side, the assistants must drop the lunge lines in case he gets tangled in them, but you can return the horse to position one and start all over again and even the most stubborn horse will give in if you allow him time and don't try to hurry him into the trailer. The worst thing you can possibly do is to lose your temper, or lose your cool.

If your horse is difficult to load, hook up your trailer and either bring it into the indoor arena, or position it in some other convenient and safe spot with good footing, and load your horse every single day before feeding him his breakfast. As soon as he is in the trailer, make a fuss of him and give him his feed. After fifteen or twenty minutes, take him out of the trailer and put him back in his stall. You will be surprised at how quickly he becomes a good loader.

Unloading is important too

A word about unloading might be appropriate. Many trailers require the horse to back out. This is not particularly difficult for the horse once he knows what to do about it, but it may become a source of difficulty or fear if the horse is allowed to "run" out backwards. He must be made to step quietly back and straight down the ramp, or down the step, if it is a step in type trailer. It takes a little more time and the aid of a calm and competent assistant to ensure that your horse learns this lesson, but it is well worth the effort when you are off somewhere on your own and you know your horse will walk straight into his trailer, and unload just as calmly when you get home.

Once a young horse has been properly introduced to loading and travelling there should be no further trouble and it should become a normal part of his routine. However, his future behaviour will also depend to some extent on his experiences when he is inside the trailer. It is very important to drive sensibly when towing a trailer. Take corners slowly and smoothly, and do not drive too fast so that you throw the horse around inside the trailer. Not only will this probably frighten him, but it may also cause him some injury.

As with all training, common sense and patience will pay off, whether you are teaching your horse to travel, or to carry you to hounds safely and boldly.

19   *Putting Your Horse 'On the Bit'*

I cannot think of any term in the horse world that is more mis-understood than putting the horse 'on the bit'. So many people talk about it in such a confused way, that it is a wonder we ever see any horses at all going correctly on the bit. And yet it is really a very simple thing.

What is 'on the bit'

One of the most common misconceptions about 'on the bit' is that it has to do solely with the position of the horse's head and neck and that it is achieved with the reins. Superficially, the position of the horse's head and neck is perhaps the most obvious feature of a horse who is going 'on the bit' for his neck will be more or less raised from the wither, depending on the collection or extension of the pace, and his head remains steady with the straight line made by the horse's forehead and nose, pointing slightly forward of an imaginary vertical line. But being 'on the bit' is very much more than a position of the horse's head and neck, and is, in fact, entirely dependent on the correct action of the back end of the horse, and not on something the rider does with the reins at all.

A horse is said to be 'on the bit' when his hocks are active and brought well under him, his topline is therefore lengthened and his weight brought somewhat off the forehand and transferred to the hindquarters, his head and neck are more or less raised from the withers with the head held steady, flexed from the poll, with the front line of the face just in front of the vertical. The bit is held lightly by the horse, with a relaxed jaw. The contact on the reins is light and steady and the horse offers no resistance to the rider's demands whether they are for changes of pace or direction.

The above describes the physical appearance of 'on the bit' but it means even more than this. Being 'on the bit' also describes a horse's psychological attitude of being obediently ready to comply with the slightest aid of the rider. Being 'on the bit' is the confirm-ation that the horse is completely obedient to the rider and is ready for absolute forward movement. By 'absolute forward movement' I mean that the horse's energies must all be ready to be exerted forwards and that the rider must 'feel' this forward tendency in the horse, even at halt and during the rein back. If this forward tendency is lacking, even if the position of the head and neck appears superficially correct, the horse is not 'on the bit' but 'behind the bit'.

How to put the horse 'on the bit'

If you study the above paragraphs carefully you will realise that the horse comes 'on the bit' quite naturally and normally as a result of correct training. Up until this stage we have asked the horse to travel with a light constant contact, in a fairly 'long' shape. We have asked him to relax his jaw and to develop his balance so that he can remain balanced and steady when performing large turns and circles and throughout transitions from one pace to another. Now we are going to ask for more from the horse. We are going to ask him to bring his haunches under him, transfer some of his weight off his forehand onto the haunches, thus lightening the forehand, and lastly we are asking for a constant state of attentive obedience to the rider's aids.

At first we do not ask the horse to remain 'on the bit' for long periods of time together, since it is tiring for him, both mentally and physically, and we must give the muscles of his loins and neck time to develop, but our ultimate aim is a schooled horse who travels 'on the bit' all the time, except when given a loose rein by the rider and encouraged to relax and stretch his neck and back.

You will see that all the training you have been doing so far, is aimed at putting the horse 'on the bit'. Provided your horse will accept a light contact with the bit and will perform circles, turns and changes of direction and pace without resistance, you can put him 'on the bit' and continue his work gradually increasing the length of time you ask him to maintain this state of alert and energetic readiness.

Actually placing the horse 'on the bit' is achieved by the combined effect of legs and hands. If the horse travels with his head too high and his back hollow, he cannot come 'on the bit' because his hind legs cannot come underneath him until he relaxes his back. The first thing to do is to 'ask' him to bring his head down. This cannot be done by force but is achieved by working the horse, usually in trot, on a large circle and maintaining a light but firm contact with the rein on the 'soft' side of the horse's mouth no matter which direction you are going, and applying squeezing and relaxing pressure on the other rein, combined with the use of your legs, working in rhythm with the horse's stride to maintain forward impulsion.

The 'soft' side of the horse is the side to which the horse bends more easily. His muscles on that side are slightly shorter than those on the resisting side, and must be stretched and lengthened until both sides of the horse are developed equally. Until this is done the horse will not go 'straight' and until he is straight he cannot go 'on the bit'.

Asking the horse to bring his head down, and then making sure that he keeps it down in all paces, is only the first step to putting him 'on the bit'. Some horses, on the other hand, carry their heads too low and must first be 'asked' to raise the head. The rider must push the horse's head up, by the action of his legs, which drive the hind legs of the horse more under him. The hands then work in much the same way as with the horse who carries his head too high. On no account should you try to 'pull' the horse's head either up or down by force, or with your hands. Pulling his head up would only result in the neck and back being hollowed, and the hocks thus prevented from coming underneath the horse, so he could not be brought 'on the bit' in this way. Trying to pull the horse's head down, by force or the use of gadgets, is equally fruitless because as soon as the force is removed the head returns to the original position.

Difficulties in putting the horse 'on the bit'

The hands must always be used with great sympathy and gentleness. Nearly all evasions of the bit are due to the horse's fear of too severe a hand. The hand alone can achieve nothing, it must be used in combination with the seat and legs. One of the most common difficulties encountered by riders attempting to put their horses 'on the bit' is that because the rider is not *sitting* correctly on the horse, with his weight on his seat bones, his driving aids are ineffective and the horse remains hollow-backed. Always look first to yourself for the solution of any problems. Make quite certain that you are sitting correctly, deep in the centre of the saddle, with your weight firmly on your seat bones, and that you do not tip forward or hollow your back as you try to send the horse forward.

Maintaining cadence

Throughout all your work it is very important to remember that the
horse must maintain an even cadence with a long, elastic, active
but controlled pace. Should he quicken his pace or shorten his stride
—which often happens in changing bend or direction, bring him
back to a slower pace and correct the rhythm with less impulsion,
and *then* gradually ask for more impulsion and a lengthened stride.
It is the rider's back and seat which primarily obtain this increase
of length of stride and not the lower leg. Using too much lower leg
usually causes the horse to hurry his steps.

In canter, particularly, there is a real danger that the horse will
not bring the hindlegs sweeping under the body as he should, but will
develop a shortened, stilted stride behind, if the rider does not keep
his seat well in the saddle and use his back to drive the hindlegs under
the horse. This shortened stride behind in canter can also be the
result of asking for 'collection' too soon. At first the canter should
be brisk and long and there should be only short periods of asking
for a shortened canter, followed immediately by driving the horse
strongly forward into a lengthened canter.

If the horse starts to 'lie' on the bit he must be corrected by a
series of half-halts, which we will discuss in detail in the next chapter
—but the rider must never use roughness or force with the hands
to try to achieve the desired lightness in canter, or any other pace.
To be effective this lightness must be obtained by the use of the seat.

What 'on the bit' is NOT

As we have seen, being 'on the bit' involves a very *light* contact on
the reins, but the horse nevertheless holds himself together and ready
balanced to obey the lightest aid of his rider. So being 'on the bit'
does NOT mean that the horse is exerting a strong pull on the
rider's hands. In the initial stages of 'asking' the horse to come 'on
the bit' there may be resistance which is shown by the horse taking
too strong a hold of the bit, but the signal that he has come 'on the
bit' is the very giving up of this strong hold. It takes two to pull, so do
not ride round and round pulling at your horse's mouth and imagine
that you are putting him 'on the bit'. It is necessary to drive the
horse forward and at the same time to 'ask' him to drop his nose and
relax his jaw, and for a few moments he may display resistance and
take too strong a feel on the reins. If this is continued for any

prolonged period of time you will know that something is wrong and you must start again.

To be correctly 'on the bit' the horse must be calm. An excited horse cannot be 'on the bit'. If his excitement is something more than a momentary reaction to some sudden outside cause, for example a car suddenly appearing, or a bird flying up from a hedge, etc., and is continued throughout his work, then something is wrong and you must look for the cause, first of all in yourself and in your riding.

Impulsion and speed

I have said that the horse 'on the bit' should move actively forward and that the rider should 'feel' the forward tendency in the horse at all times. Do not confuse this energetic forward tendency with rushing about. The horse who is calmly 'on the bit' moves forward with rhythmic, energetic strides, but how often does one see horses rushing hurriedly along, particularly in trot, simply 'running'. The riders obviously think that their horse is full of 'impulsion' but they are confusing 'impulsion' and 'speed'.

Impulsion is the willingness of the horse to go freely forward at whatever pace the rider wishes on his command. Speed is confused with impulsion because certainly the horse is going forward—but he is hurrying and his energies are not controlled as they are in the balanced horse, full of impulsion. The horse who is hurried along too fast, without proper regard for rhythm and cadence, is usually frightened, either of the rider's overstrong legs or his rough hands. He is not relaxed and calm and calmness is the first objective of all schooling.

A good seat—which includes, of course, good hands and sympathetic application of the aids—brings calmness and steadiness to the horse. Once the horse is put 'on the bit' and taught the correct way of going, his impulsion can be gradually increased without shortening his stride or hurrying his pace, by increased use of the rider's back and seat.

Evasions

Roughness with the hand will lead to a frightened horse who remains 'over the bit' and inattentive. Too strong a hand, and a lack of understanding about the part played by the haunches can lead to a false position of the horse's head, with the neck bent at the third or fourth vertebra instead of at the poll, and the chin tucked in to his chest. This is known as either 'over the bit' or 'behind the bit'.

The horse 'on the bit' is virtually a 'prisoner' held between the rider's seat and his hands. In order to escape the horse must first give up contact with the bit, either by coming above it, or behind it. This is never done unintentionally by the horse—he does it only when he avoids or evades the rider and the forward movement. The horse will usually develop evasions only when hurried in his training or forced too quickly from one stage to another. Training should always move positively forward, but the horse must be given time to master one stage before being moved on to the next.

It is of the utmost importance for the guarantee of obedience that your horse should go 'on the bit'. The forward urge of the horse that comes with being 'on the bit' itself creates the light, elastic contact of the rider's hands, through the reins, with the bit in the horse's mouth. The reins, really, become the connection between the requesting rider and the compliant horse. In order for this to come about the horse must be calm, willing and attentive. So long as this elastic contact between the horse's mouth and the rider's hand exists, the horse is 'on the bit'.

20 *More Suppling Exercises: Half-halts, Circles, and Shoulder-in*

It is only by making the horse supple that we can enable him to come correctly 'on the bit', move correctly round corners, and 'use' himself properly, 'swinging' his back and bringing his hind legs actively under himself, directly behind the forehand. If the horse is ever to go beyond the most basic level of training, all this is necessary.

We teach the horse to move properly, to 'swing' his back, to keep his quarters directly behind his forehand and not allow them to swing out on circles and turns, and therefore enable him to perform the many complex and demanding tasks we ask of the trained horse, by constant use of suppling gymnastic exercises.

Suppling from front to rear (longitudinal)

To supple the horse longitudinally—i.e. from front to rear, we can use half-halts, full halts, and, later on, the rein back.

The half-halt, which is also known as 'rebalancing' the horse, a term I prefer because it is more descriptive of our goal, is the first longitudinal suppling exercise we teach, apart from using trotting poles, or cavaletti, which do, to a certain extent, supple the horse lengthwise. What we want the horse to do in the half-halt, is to bring his haunches more underneath him and to move his point of balance back, thus lightening the forehand and raising it slightly.

The half-halt is achieved in exactly the same way as you achieve walk from trot, for example, except that, just at the moment when the horse is about to break into a walk, you drive him forward again with your seat and resume the trot.

Half-halts are used mainly at trot and canter, and it is very important to use a strong seat and very light hand. Start at the trot, on a large circle. Sit to the trot and establish a good, active swinging trot. Then decide where you are going to make your half-halt, sit deeper and use both legs to send the hind-quarters forward, under the horse, and at the same time close the fingers of the outside hand and do not allow the horse to move forward from the pressure of the seat and legs. The responsive horse will rebalance himself to the rear and prepare to break into a walk, and exactly at that moment, the fingers yield and permit him to trot forward again in the same rhythm. It is important at first to use one hand actively and allow the other simply to keep in light contact with the bit. If you use both hands you may well end up pulling, and the horse will probably resist and throw his head up, hollowing his back—exactly what you don't want him to do. Even a green horse is unlikely to do this if you ask for the half-halt with only one hand.

Use half-halts on a circle, and also in the track as you go around the school. Another good way to use them is to turn across the school from one long side to the opposite side, making a right-angled turn around the haunches, and half-halt as you cross the centre. Always turn to the opposite direction on the far side of the school. Vary the exercise, and sometimes ask for a full-halt on the centre and sometimes a half-halt. You can also practise half-halts and halts along the centre line, coming from one short side of the school to the other.

Half-halts need not be restricted to your work in the school. Use them as you work outside—particularly trotting down long, fairly gentle hills. But always be very careful to achieve the rebalancing with your seat and use your hand very lightly indeed.

Circular tracks

It is now time to be much more demanding of your horse on circles and circular tracks, including riding through the corners of the school. The riding of circular tracks is probably one of the most important of all training exercises. Going round a circle the horse must bend his spine to comply with the direction of the movement. This is not easy, as from the withers to the quarters the horse has little lateral flexibility. The muscles of the loins are developed considerably by work on the circle since they are stretched and contracted in turn depending on the direction of the circle. Knowing the importance of these muscles to the action of the horse's quarters, that is, his impulsion, the advantages of improving and developing them becomes obvious.

On the circle, if the horse is kept correctly bent around the perimeter, with his hind feet following directly the track of his forefeet and the quarters not being permitted to fall in or fall out, it is obvious that the inside legs must take a slightly shorter step than the outside legs, which have further to travel. At the walk, which is a pace of four time when each foot comes to the ground separately, this presents little problem, but at the trot, which is a two beat gait when the legs are used in diagonally opposite pairs, the difficulties are increased because the inside hind leg, which must take a slightly shorter step, is used with the outside front leg, which must take a slightly longer step; and vice versa. This discrepancy is very slight on a large circle, but becomes much more important on a small circle. This is why it is so hard to ride a small circle correctly in trot. The horse's balance and rhythm will be affected, and to perform the small circle correctly will require considerable adjustment of stride and rhythm, considerable bending, and great effort from the horse.

At this stage you should keep your circles fairly large, not less than about 15 metres, reducing gradually over a period of some months to about 10 metres. However, it is easy to appreciate that the circle, and the circular tracks are themselves truly demanding physical exercises for the horse, if performed correctly.

When riding circles, remember that you are not only asking the horse to contract the muscles along that side of his body which is to the inside of the circle, but you are also asking him to stretch the muscles along the outside of his body. If, in asking for the circle, you keep the horse moving actively forward, in front of your seat and legs, and on the bit, you will not, in fact, have to 'ask' for the circle with the inside rein at all, but simply yield a little with the outside rein. By 'yield a little with the outside rein' I mean simply relax the fingers of the outside hand slightly—on no account 'throw away' the contact with the outside rein. This yielding will be sufficient perhaps with the addition of a *very* light touch of the outside rein against his neck, to position him round the circle, without the danger that the inside rein, however carefully used, may act as an indirect rein of opposition and force the quarters to fall out from the circle. The horse should automatically stretch the side of his neck and body on which you yield, and lower his head slightly, in his search to maintain contact with the bit. In other words, try bending your horse round the circle by inviting him to stretch the outside of his body and bend *himself* round the circle, instead of by using a direct rein aid to the inside to make him bend round the circle, which may also have the effect of throwing the quarters out.

This slightly different way of applying the aids for a circle can be a very effective way of improving and refining your riding round circles and circular tracks, and has the added advantage that it encourages the horse to lower his head slightly and search downwards for the bit, whereas a direct rein aid can have the effect of 'forcing' the horse onto the circle and creating resistances in the horse which need never arise.

Before the horse can derive full benefit from the work on circular tracks he must first be fairly steadily on the bit. Riding the circles, loops and serpentines in the way I have described above will also avoid any sort of backward pull on both reins. This backward pull is what destroys the horse's rhythm, impulsion and also his bend, and is the main reason why circles are so often performed badly.

Lateral suppling

Initially, the best exercise to use to supple the horse laterally, is the shoulder-in. The shoulder-in, in its perfect form, is a movement on two tracks, but it is preferable to begin it with much less bend and to

Shoulder-in

perform it at first as a movement on three tracks. The horse is flexed throughout his whole length away from the direction in which he is moving. That is, if the horse is flexed to the left, (left shoulder-in), he is actually moving to his own right. In this position, the left front and left hind are called the inside legs and the right front and the right hind the outside legs.

The shoulder-in makes great demands on the inside legs, particularly the inside hind leg, which has to move deeply forward under the horse and carry most of the weight in a flexed position. The flexion of the shoulder-in, away from the direction in which the horse is actually moving, is the same as the natural flexion assumed by a horse making a free turn on his centre. This explains why this exercise, which is the only lateral movement where the horse is flexed away from the direction in which he is moving, comes easily to the horse and is the most suitable two track exercise to use at first.

Free forward movement and maintaining impulsion

The shoulder-in may be performed on straight lines; round the entire school, including the corners, which are a quarter of a circle; and ultimately on the circle itself. The angle at which the horse is maintained must never be more than 30° to 45°, and to start with should

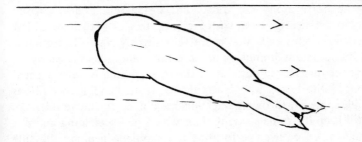

be NO MORE THAN 15°. If the angle is too great, the amount of bend will impede the free forward movement of the horse, and the whole object of all exercises, and particularly all lateral exercises, is the ultimate improvement of free forward movement by the supplling and strengthening of the energetic action of the hocks.

Never let this basic rule leave your mind, and as you practice lateral work, constantly remind yourself that the free and energetic action of the hock is just as important as the freedom of the shoulder.

At the start, teach the shoulder-in to your horse in walk. In fact, shoulder-in is usually practised in trot, the pace which best enables the rider to maintain the free forward movement, rhythm and impulsion of the horse, but it is no good trying to do it at trot if the horse does not understand what is wanted. At first the horse will resist and try to avoid making the necessary physical effort to place his inside hind leg both forward and sideways. This exercise, even with only 15° of bend and performed in walk, requires considerable physical effort from the horse and just as we ourselves are inclined to try to avoid demands for increased muscular effort, the horse will try to avoid making the necessary effort to bring his inside hind leg well forward.

Begin the shoulder-in from a circle. Ride your horse round a fairly large circle at first, create in him the correct bend, around the circle, and the correct rhythm. You start from walk but do not allow the horse to 'slop' along, put him together and walk actively, thinking about collecting his energies, making sure that the inside hind leg is active. Choose the spot at which you are going to leave the circle and proceed in shoulder-in. The most usual place to do this would be along the wall, or the track, of your school. When the horse's quarters reach this point, push him away sideways, along the tangent to the circle. The aids are simple, both legs working in rhythm with the horse's stride with the inside leg strongest, and the outside rein to 'lead' the horse along the track. The inside rein is also carried slightly in the direction you wish the horse to go—in the case of left shoulder-in, both hands will move very slightly right. The outside leg helps maintain impulsion if necessary, and remains ready to prevent the quarters falling out of the track, which is quite a usual evasion of the horse who is trying to avoid bending his rather inflexible spine. By throwing the haunches out, he can move sideways and still keep his spine straight. This would be leg yielding and not shoulder-in. Of course, performing the shoulder-in along the side of the school where you have a wall or fence, helps to prevent this particular evasion by the horse.

When the horse has taken the required number of steps at shoulder-in, send him forwards again on a fairly large circle. In the beginning, ask only four or five steps at shoulder-in before re-taking your circle. When the horse has gained strength and suppleness, you can ask for longer and longer stretches at shoulder-in.

The rhythm of the steps, the pace of the horse, and the amount of impulsion, must be exactly the same at the shoulder-in as they were on the circle. Do not allow the horse to slow down or shorten his stride when moving from the circle into shoulder-in. Do not allow him either, to bend only the neck and keep his body straight. The bend must be absolutely uniform throughout the entire length of the horse.

The inside hind leg is asked to make a tremendously increased effort in shoulder-in, since it is obliged to tread both forwards under the horse and also sideways. To start with, the horse will try to avoid the necessary increase of the flexion of the hock. He will be unable to do it, so he must try to evade it at first. His evasion will be shown by loss of rhythm and impulsion and by clumsiness. Immediately this loss of rhythm happens, re-take the circle, re-establish your rhythm, hock action, and impulsion, and then try again.

At first you must be satisfied with very little. If you get one or two good steps it is sufficient. You re-take the circle and then try again for one or two good steps, and then again re-take the circle.

As soon as the horse understands what is required, practice the shoulder-in in trot rather than in walk. It is easy to lose impulsion in walk, and the horse can also learn to come behind the bit and even to collect himself against the rider. This is less likely to happen with the active forward movement of the trot.

There are several exercises incorporating the shoulder-in and the circle; for example, make a circle about 10 metres in one corner of the school, move along the short side in shoulder-in and re-take the circle in the next corner. Leave the circle in shoulder-in until you are half way down the long side of the school and then re-take the circle. Again shoulder-in to the next corner, circle in the corner and shoulder-in along the short end of the arena, and so on, all the way round the school. Remember, always practice every exercise equally to the right and the left. Try asking a few steps of extended trot as you change the rein across the diagonal, you will be surprised how readily your horse answers your demand for a lengthened stride after he has been made to flex and strengthen his hock joints.

Passing through corners in shoulder-in

Once the horse is proficient at the shoulder-in on a straight line, continue in shoulder-in all the way round the arena, including passing through the corners. To pass through the corner correctly at shoulder-in remember that the quarters must finish the corner at the exact spot where the forehand started it. This means that if you are moving

along the long side in shoulder-in and are to pass through the corner
and continue along the short end still in shoulder-in, when the forehand reached the track along the short side the horse must be sent
on a purely circular track for exactly one length. When his quarters
reach the spot where his forehand started the circular track, he is
side-stepping again. In the same way, if you wish to start the shoulder-
in from a straight track—which may be done once the horse understands the exercise—the correct way to do so is to commence a
circle and as soon as the quarters reach the spot where the forehand
left the track, you begin the shoulder-in.

Shoulder-in on the circle

Performing the shoulder-in round the circle demands a great deal
from the horse. Obviously, the smaller the circle the more difficult
the exercise becomes. When the horse is really active and supple and
is able to move at shoulder-in with impulsion and perfect rhythm,
the shoulder-in may be practised on the circle. The horse is kept at an
angle of 20° to 30° but never more than 45° even for the fully trained
horse, with the tangent to the circle. The forehand moves round an
inner circle and the quarters move round an outer circle, both
circles being concentric.

The benefits of shoulder-in

The particular benefits of shoulder-in are the demands it makes on
the inside legs, shoulder, loins, hip and elbow and particularly on
the inside hock. The shoulder-in on the circle is beneficial for
increasing the mobility of the quarters, hips, elbows and hocks. It
also stretches the loins somewhat.

Extending the Stride in Trot

Much of the training of any horse is done in trot. This is partly because the trot is a pace in two-time and is the most regular of all the horse's gaits. The horse can trot using his hocks naturally and lightening the forehand, carrying his head fairly high, and still. Because he springs from one diagonal pair of legs to the other in even rhythm, he does not need to move his head in order to balance himself as he does in walk. and to a lesser degree, in canter.

Developing rhythm and cadence

Wynmalen says that 'rhythm is the father of cadence. So by concentrating on rhythm, cadence will, in the end, come all by itself, and with it perfection.' The trot, being by nature absolutely rhythmic, it follows that it is of great value for the athletic development of the horse.

During most of the early training of the horse, the trot is performed rising. There are no hard and fast rules about when you should rise to the trot and when you should sit, but if you ride correctly you will be able to achieve exactly the same use of the seat whether you are rising or sitting, and there is absolutely no advantage in sitting to the trot if the horse has not reached a stage of training where he really swings his back. Sitting will simply prove uncomfortable for both horse and rider and therefore is likely to disturb the harmony between them. When rising to the trot, of course, the rider must alternate the diagonal, riding first on one diagonal pair of legs and then on the other. In the school, the generally accepted rule is to ride on the outside diagonal, this means that the rider's seat comes into the saddle as the outside front and inside hind legs strike the ground. But whether you ride on the inside diagonal or the outside, be consistent and change the diagonal each time you change direction or your horse will become stiff and one sided.

Correct seat and the use of the hand

What many riders fail to realise is the damage that can be done by too strong a use of the hand. In fact, at trot, the rider does very little. Because the horse holds his head still, and the trot is a very regular gait, the rider's hands can stay almost completely still. The rider should sit still and 'supervise and encourage' the horse in his natural rhythm. The most certain way to disturb the progress is interference with the horse's mouth.

If your horse is not going calmly, on the bit, with good rhythm after you have thoroughly and quietly worked your way through the system of training described in previous chapters, then you must ask yourself what has been wrong with your training so far. It may be that you are stiff yourself, or that you are not sitting correctly, well down on your seat bones with your legs long and relaxed and neither too far back nor too far forward. It may be that you are using too strong a hand, or insufficient seat and legs to balance your hand, or it may be that your aids have not been sufficiently clear. This self-criticism is very important, particularly for the rider who must work alone without the advantage of an instructor. Nearly all faults in the rider are traceable to an incorrect seat, and nearly all problems in horses are cured by the rider 'sitting correctly'. Probably the most common fault seen watching any group of riders, is a tendency to hollow the back and tip forward off the seat bones, at the same time allowing the lower leg to slip back. Sitting perched in this position it is absolutely impossible to send the horse freely forward in any gait.

If things aren't going right, get an honest and observant friend to watch you ride, and be prepared to admit in your own mind that it is possible for you to have slipped into some bad habits in your riding.

Lengthening the stride in trot

We are now ready to begin developing the trot, which eventually should become easily variable from the maximum extension to the maximum collection, all with perfect cadence. We start, not with collection, but with lengthening, because of the danger of slowing the horse down and simply loosing all free forward movement. When starting to lengthen the stride in trot, we use the rising trot. Sitting would probably be uncomfortable for both horse and rider, and in any case, rising during the beginnings of this work will encourage the horse's impulsion.

First establish a good ordinary trot, that means a trot with longish strides and an even tempo. The head should be still, with a light even contact on the mouth and the front of the face at an angle of about 45° in front of the verticle. As you come round the short end of the arena, shorten the trot slightly, gathering the horse together, but keeping the same rhythm. Turn down the long side of the arena about a yard in from the track and using both legs just enough to demand increased energy and, initially, increased speed, rise slightly higher, and very slightly lower your hand.

When you ask the horse to go faster in trot, the initial effect will be for him to drive harder with his hind legs, and the first two or three strides will be longer than previously. If you allow him to continue, the length of the strides will probably diminish and he will simply take shorter, faster strides, and this is what you do not want to happen. So, at first, you ask only four or five strides in the lengthened trot, and then bring him back to an ordinary trot again. Be very careful to bring the horse back gently. The feeling should be that of 'receiving' his increased energy into your hand, cease driving with your legs, and bring the horse quietly to his ordinary trot.

Be very light with your aids and ask only for very little at a time. Be sure to prepare the horse before making the demand for increased energy, by gathering him together slightly at first. Never be rough and always be certain that you retain the even rhythm of the trot.

Practise this increase of speed, receiving the horse on the bit, holding him softly on the bit for one or two lengthened strides, then retarding him to his ordinary trot, all the time maintaining an even rhythm, both in the arena and outdoors. You will find that the horse gradually becomes more supple, will flex more and will be brought back on his hocks just a little bit each time. This will eventually lead to better balance and lightness and ultimately to collection.

When to try lengthening the trot

A very good time to practise lengthening the stride in trot is after working at shoulder-in. The shoulder-in exercise makes the horse more active with his hocks, obliging him to step deeply under with the inside hind leg in a flexed position. If you bring the horse round a corner in shoulder-in, for example, and then move across the diagonal at rising trot, asking for increased impulsion and therefore length of stride, you will find it very easy to get the horse to exert his energies forward. This is also a good way to start to associate the rising trot with extension in the horse's mind which itself can be very useful, since the act of rising can then become an aid by association and can help the rider to maintain the impulsion during training at some moments when it might otherwise be difficult.

This does not mean that you ALWAYS rise to the extended trot. Once the horse has learnt that you want him to lengthen his stride and cover more ground, not to speed up his pace, and you can trot in good rhythm, lengthen the strides, receive the horse on the bit, slow him down, even to a little slower than his normal trot, still maintaining an absolutely even rhythm, he will be supple enough for the rider to sit comfortably during these lengthenings and shortenings. At sitting trot the rider is more closely in touch with the horse and, of course, can use his back as a driving aid. At the sitting trot the rider can also concentrate much more on the horse's responsiveness and work towards achieving a cadence, through absolute rhythm coupled with impulsion, during slight variations of pace. You must progress very slowly and carefully in this work, never asking more from the horse than he is able to give, or you may spoil his rhythm. If the work is correct, you will feel the horse's back gradually soften and his mouth becoming more responsive and educated.

Work on the circle can be a great help in achieving greater impulsion since the horse really has to deliver more energy with the inside hind leg when he is moving on a circle. Be sure to work equally to both directions on the circle, unless the horse is already one sided, in which case the circle can be used to help develop the weaker diagonal. Working outside as well as in the arena will also help to achieve more impulsion.

Transitions and half-halts

Transitions from trot to walk and walk to trot, and later from trot to halt, and halt to trot are also valuable exercises. All transitions should be gradual—there should be no sudden jerk to a stop. In coming from trot to walk the trot should gradually subside into a walk, the head should be held steady and never be thrown up in transitions either from trot to walk or from walk to trot. At first the horse will need several strides in which to lose the impulsion of

The author on *The Englishman*. This horse is 'on the bit' in a collected walk. The stride has been shortened and elevated, the top line of the horse lengthened, the haunches brought more underneath the body, and the head and neck more or less raised from the withers and relaxed at the poll. The degree of collection will increase as the training progresses. The horse can be 'on the bit' and NOT collected. But he cannot be collected without being 'on the bit'. At the moment the photograph was taken the rider was 'asking' with slightly more than should be consistently maintained. Ideally, the contact should be only the weight of the rein (Chapter 19). *Photo Nancy Bizzarro*

The shoulder in. Dominique Barbier on *Don Pasquale* (Chapter 20). *Photo Francine Halkin*

The author on *Don Rossio*. Right shoulder in on the circle. The horse is active, light and moving freely, crossing his legs well. He is very slightly overbent but this problem will be easily corrected by slightly increased use of rider's seat and legs (Chapter 20). *Photo Nancy Bizzarro*

Extending the stride at trot, sitting (Chapter 21)

The author on *Don Rossio*. Extending the stride at trot must come from increased energy and drive from the hind quarters. Note the tremendous activity behind (Chapter 21). *Photo Nancy Bizzarro*

The author on *Don Rossio*, a Lusitano stallion. A sequence of four photographs showing the right turn on the haunches (Chapter 23). *Photos Nancy Bizzarro*

1   Collecting the walk in preparation for the turn, rider leads horse into turn with right hand at the same time holding haunches with left leg

2   Horse walks forehand around haunches. Hind feet are picked up and replaced on same spot, keeping the rhythm of the walk

3 Completing the turn. Notice that the movement is always forward and that the hind feet are picked up and not pivoted in place

4 After completing the turn the horse walks forward still maintaining exactly the same pace and rhythm. Notice the relaxed and attentive position of the horse's head, his mouth is closed and moist, his ears 'listening' to his rider

Half pass to the left (Chapter 23)

A balanced canter through a right handed corner (Chapter 24)

Mary Rose on the Lusitano stallion, *Achille*, in Spanish Walk. *Photo Francine Halkin*

Cross-country jumping: jumping up a bank. Mary Rose on *The Englishman* winning the
Preliminary Division at West Hampden Training Stables 3 Phase Event in June 1975

the trot and establish the walk. As he improves in balance and suppleness, he will be able to make the transitions with fewer intervening strides, and eventually without loss of impulsion and with no intervening strides. Eventually the horse should make all his transitions, up and down, maintaining impulsion, coming from a collected, impulsive trot into a lively, collected walk, but this will take many months of work to achieve, and great lightness and sensitivity from the rider.

The half-halt, particularly used on a circular track, either in making a complete circle, or in making a serpentine down the full length of the school, can be enormously helpful. The half-halt is really a calling of the horse to attention. The rider says to him 'Now listen, pay attention and balance yourself, we are going to do something different' so the horse gradually learns to carry himself balanced, supple and attentive, and yet deliver the required energy to keep up his impulsion.

The halt

Finally, a word about the halt. It is important that the horse should learn from the start to halt correctly, with his weight evenly balanced on all four legs. Many horses have difficulty doing this and consistently leave one hind leg behind, so failing to complete the stride with their front legs. The answer to the problem is practice. Endless walking and halting, making sure that the halt is square. If you cannot feel if the horse is standing square and you have no friend along to help you, let us hope that you either have a mirror or that the sun is shining so that you can glance at the horse's shadow on the ground.

The horse should come to a correct halt, stand balanced and ready, and move off when told with energy and suppleness, and without throwing his head during the transition. If he does have a tendency to throw his head up you may be sure you are using rather too strong a hand. Try using more seat, a definite holding with the thighs, and only the inside hand and that lightly. Using both hands equally is almost guaranteed to make a green horse throw up his head, so avoid that, and never, never use the hand without the back, the seat and the leg.

The halt

Once your horse has achieved a certain degree of balance it becomes important that each time he halts, he should halt effectively. That is to say, not simply come to a stand still just anyhow, unbalanced, hind legs left behind, crooked, or leaning on the bit. He must halt correctly, from the back end to the front end. The quarters should be slightly lowered, the horse should remain balanced, keeping his head and neck in place and giving slightly with his lower jaw. He should bring his forelegs into position under him so that he is standing up square, attentive, and ready to obey the rider's next command.

The importance of concentration

Achieving correct halts, even from the earliest training, is a question of tact and patience, especially with a highly strung horse.

It is important to remember that you ride the horse first and foremost with your head. When you are riding the horse in walk, for example, you follow his movement with your seat and hands and you think about the kind of walk you want. the rhythm, the length of stride, and the amount of impulsion. You 'permit' him to walk by following his movement. If you wish to shorten the length of steps taken you think about the shorter steps and 'follow the horse slightly less' with your seat and hands. If you wish to lengthen the steps taken, you think of the longer stride and 'follow the horse more' with your seat and hands. When you wish to make the horse halt, you think of the halt you want and stop your seat and hands from moving. It is as simple as that. Think about coming to a halt, and then stop your seat and hands from following the movements of the horse. He will come to a halt too.

Lightness of the rein aid

It is very important not to pull on the reins. If your aim is to have a pleasant, light, obedient and enjoyable horse to ride then you must teach him to be this way from the very beginning and you must never, never pull back on the reins. This is not to say that you never create resistance with the reins, but you must do it by bringing your shoulders slightly back and then closing the fingers and ceasing to give with the hand, and NOT by pulling backwards with your hands.

Try the halt from walk as I have described it, simply by thinking about the halt and ceasing to follow the horse with your seat and hands. It works, and it is so much easier and more effective than trying to use the reins as a brake. Right from the start the horse begins to learn to listen to your seat. The best trained horse is the one who needs no hands, no legs, only the seat and his rider's mind.

Obtaining square halts

It is easy to teach any horse to halt from the walk in the way I have described, but the halts will not always be very correct—one hind leg may be left behind, or he may not be square in front. Using this method as a base, however, you can gradually begin to ask for more precision in the halt by the very gentle and gradual use of your lower leg. You should have the feeling of 'riding your horse forward into the halt'. He should halt from the back end forwards. That is, your seat and legs should halt his hindquarters (the engine) and your hands permit his forehand to complete the stride, but no more, so that he stands up square, balanced, and attentive.

Above all, the halt must be still! This seems obvious but it is surprising how many people struggle to make correct halts before their horse has learned to stop and stand still until told by his rider to move. Use your voice a great deal at this stage, and stroke the horse to reassure him that he is doing the right thing. The more highly strung he is the more patience you will require. Once he has learned to halt and stand still without trying to escape in any way, then you can work towards correcting and perfecting the halt.

Transitions and rhythm

Practice moving off from halt into walk, as well as coming from walk to halt, and be acutely aware of the rhythm of the walk. Keep the same rhythm after the halt that you had before it, and do not allow the horse to escape through changing his rhythm.

Once you have achieved really good halts and departs from walk, practice halting from the trot, and moving forward into the same rhythm trot after three or four seconds. This exercise is vital in the training of any horse and is one of the means of obtaining correct collection.

The horse should come into a halt with his back soft, his hindquarters slightly lowered, in such a way that the rider feels the effects of this softness in his saddle, and not a jolting action.

Gradually increase the time you ask the horse to remain immobile. If he is nervous and restless, try practicing halts right at the end of your schooling time. He will quickly learn that if he stands still satisfactorily, you will dismount and he will have finished his work. Ask only for a brief halt before dismounting at first, and gradually lengthen the time you require the horse to remain still. A properly trained horse must stand perfectly still for as long as his rider wishes, no matter what is happening around him.

Once your horse is halting satisfactorily on his own, do the same work in an arena with other horses working around you.

Finally, your horse must learn to halt and remain immobile out in the open. Nothing must make him impatient to be off until his rider tells him to move.

The rein back

I believe in teaching the rein back fairly early in the horse's schooling. Correctly performed the rein back will in no way endanger the forward obedience of the horse. Many authorities teach that the rein back is dangerous and that if it is used early in his training a horse will learn to run backwards as an evasion. This most certainly would be the case if the rein back was obtained or performed incorrectly or if it was abused instead of used.

The rein back is not natural to a horse. although every horse can do it easily when he needs to. At liberty, the horse will always try to turn round to escape from a tight spot rather than step back, and when he does step back he does not use the four beat time of a walk, but the two beat diagonal motion of the trot.

Explain, do not force

It is very simple to teach your horse to rein back correctly if you start out by explaining to him what you want instead of trying to force him into it. Stand on the ground in front of your horse and tell him to 'back' as you step deliberately towards him. You may use your whip to tap him gently on his chest at the same time, or you may press your toe very gently on the coronet of each front foot in turn to give him the idea of what you want. Although you will be holding the reins it is very important that you do not exert any pressure on them at all. You can, indeed, make the horse go backwards by pulling him back with his bit, but this is not the rein back, it is forcing the horse to run backwards. One or two steps backwards is quite sufficient at first. Reward him, and repeat, until he fully understands.

Once you are sure your horse properly understands you from the ground, do exactly the same thing from the saddle. Give a few light taps with your whip on his chest, bring your weight very slightly forward, off your seatbones, keep your hands perfectly still and do not 'give', and say 'back'. Again, one or two steps is enough—reward, rest, and repeat the exercise.

Correct aids for rein back

The next step is to associate very gradually the correct aids with the movement, and never asking more than a step or two at a time. The way I do it is to bring the horse to a balanced halt, stand perfectly still and ask him to lower his head. This I achieve by very light use of the legs, combined with a fixed hand—not pulling, but simply resting against the shoulders and not giving. When the head drops, the horse is ready to respond to the aid to rein back. I use my legs gently again, asking him to move forwards, but I do not give with my hands—I keep them absolutely still with the fingers closed on the rein. At the same time, I bring my weight very slightly forward off my seat bones, thus 'opening the back door', and the horse steps backwards, calmly, relaxed and straight.

It is important to remember that the rein back is essentially a forward movement. You must create in your horse a forward tendency and just when he is about to move forward, close your fingers on the rein so that he exerts the forward tendency in a backward direction. The horse must always remain between your leg and your hand, and the action of your leg must always proceed and predominate over the action of your hand.

It is important to ride your horse back very carefully, step by step, and to be able to halt or move forward easily and certainly at any moment. For most horses, the rein back is only of limited value in the early training and only three or four steps should be asked at a time. However, if your horse is very heavy on his forehand and is the type who likes to support his weight on the reins, it can be a most useful and effective exercise for lightening the forehand.

The rein back as an aid to suppling and collection

In more advanced training the rein back is used to strengthen and supple the loins, haunches and hocks. In the rein back the horse is shortened from front to rear, bringing additional weight onto the hindquarters, which have to bend more in very joint, particularly the hocks. The quarters drop and all the joints are suppled. Combining the rein back with transitions into trot or canter gives you a very powerful muscular exercise and is a tremendous help in lightening the forehand and increasing the horse's impulsion.

Correctly performed by a trained horse, the rein back retains the shape and bearing of a collected movement. The horse's head will be high and bent at the poll but the face must never come behind the verticle. He will keep his head still and his mouth relaxed. There will be no appreciable tension on the reins, certainly no pull and no backward movement of the rider's hands. The rider's legs will be resting lightly on the horse's sides—they maintain the impulsion and at the same time keep the horse straight. The steps will be equal, slow and deliberate. The horse will bend his hocks and bring his hindlegs backwards in turn in a perfectly straight line. If the horse hurries backwards he will not have time to bend his hocks sufficiently and will therefore not be able to step back straight. When you are performing the rein back you must be able to halt your horse smoothly and precisely after any given number of steps backwards, or move forwards into walk, trot or canter with no hesitation, difficulty or loss of impulsion. A tall order, but one you will achieve if you proceed slowly with tact, gentleness and determination.

23 *Work on two tracks*

By this stage of your horse's training he should be going confidently forward, fairly reliably on the bit at all paces and through transitions. Now you must continue his training, aiming for an even higher standard. The horse should be light and responsive; calm, yet keen; supple, and obedient.

The way to achieve these objectives is through the gymnastic exercises on two tracks. The expression 'on two tracks' refers to movements in which the horse's hind feet follow a different track from that of his front feet. This is obviously not a natural way for the horse to progress, but it happens whenever he goes sideways, or sideways and forwards.

All your work should be aimed towards the development of even more freedom of forward movement, impulsion, more balance, more suppleness, more rhythm and increased cadence, leading to more extension and more collection. Work on two tracks, which involves the horse crossing his legs, stepping rather higher with the over-stepping legs, and bringing them forward a little more than normal, is ideal for developing the necessary elasticity and power of shoulder, thigh and loin muscles which are so important in achieving the above objectives.

Rhythm and cadence

This may be a good moment to consider the meaning of the two words 'rhythm' and 'cadence' as they are applied to the way a horse goes. Whereas rhythm consists simply of keeping correct time, cadence is keeping correct time with much greater energy. The untrained horse is incapable of cadence, because it requires so much energy—much more than the untrained horse would normally use for comparable speed. But the trained horse easily produces the maximum impulsion all the time, without effort, in all paces and movements. The whole object of his training is precisely that—to make him able to produce the maximum impulsion without strain, and remain perfectly calm and light.

Importance of the walk

All three paces are used in the training of the horse, and they complement each other. We do use the trot considerably because it is such a level gait and the horse keeps his head very still in trot in comparison with walk and canter, but the trot has the disadvantage of not being a particularly good means of suppling the horse's back, for instance, just because the horse does remain so steady, with a nearly still head carriage. So do not forget the walk and the canter, and use only the trot. The walk, in particular, is a very neglected gait, and it is important to understand just how much work you can and should do in walk, both in putting your horse on the bit, and also in teaching him to use his back.

Much of your work outside should be done in walk, and much of it in walk with a long rein. If your horse jogs, and anticipates the trot, every time you pick up the reins, this may be an indication to you that you have been neglecting the work at the walk.

With a soft, unfit, horse, also, the work at the walk can be a tremendous help in advancing the horse's training and muscling him up at the same time.

Turns on the haunches

Work on two tracks really could be said to begin with the earliest turn on the forehand and, of course, with shoulder-in which we discussed earlier. As soon as you have gained control of the hindquarters through this work, the turn on the haunches should present no difficulties.

The turn on the haunches is a simple, but most important, manoeuvre. Through the use of this turn you cannot only gain much greater control over the 'engine' of the horse (the hind quarters), but also you can start to bend and supple the haunches, and lighten the forehand. The final form of the turn on the haunches is the pirouette, or 360° turn with the haunches remaining almost in one spot, maintaining the gait on a very small circle, and the forehand describing a complete circle around them. The pirouette is performed in walk, piaffe and canter, and is a very advanced movement, beyond the scope of this present book. For information about it I would recommend the reader to study *Dressage* by Henry Wynmalen.

The beginnings of the turn on the haunches is what interests us at this stage of our horse's training. We need to make his haunches more supple and active, and lighten his forehand, and to do this we must teach him to turn his forehand around the quarters and move

Turn on the haunches

straight forward afterwards, with impulsion. This turn may be performed from the halt or from the walk, and I prefer to teach it from the walk first as I think this makes it easier for the horse to maintain the activity and rhythm of the hindlegs. At first the horse should be asked to take only one or two steps, bringing the forehand around the haunches and should then be sent immediately forwards in an active walk. Gradually, we add one more step and then another, until the horse is able to make a 90° turn and then a 180° turn, keeping up

the activity of the hindlegs in the rhythm of walk, and not pivoting on
the inside hindleg or taking any step backwards.

The aids for the turn on the haunches are simply to lead the horse
round with the inside rein, supported with the outside rein on the
neck, and push the forehand around the quarters with the outside
leg, preventing the quarters from falling out with the lower leg
and using the thigh and knee to assist in moving the shoulders over.
The inside leg stays at the girth and helps to maintain the forward
movement. Do not over-use the inside leg or you will confuse the
horse, but if it is not there at all you will lose the rhythm of the walk
and the control of the hindquarters.

Practice the turn on the haunches by walking around your school,

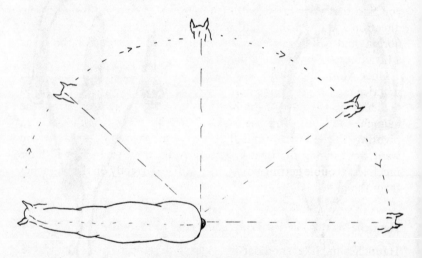

Turn on the haunches

slightly collecting the horse's energies between your hand and leg
as a preparation for the turn, then asking for one or two steps of the
forehand around the quarters and walking straight forward to a
point on the opposite side of the school and continuing round the
track in the opposite direction. Gradually increase the number
of steps you ask from your horse until you achieve a complete 180°
about turn without difficulty. If, despite the efforts of your outside
leg, you have difficulty preventing the haunches from swinging out
in the turn and the horse from turning on the centre, try asking with
the outside leg just one step before you want to make your turn. This
will have the effect of making the outside hind leg take one step

inwards, crossing in front of the inside hind leg, just before you ask his shoulders to move around his haunches, and will prevent any tendency of the haunches to swing out.

The easiest place to start your turns on the haunches is along the side of the school, so that the wall helps you in your efforts to prevent the haunches from falling out, but as soon as you are able to achieve one or two steps you should start to practice the turns on the haunches at other spots in the school, without the support of the wall. Try walking straight along the centre line and then asking for one or two steps of a right turn on the haunches, walking straight forward, and turning left into the track. Naturally, you must practice this exercise equally in both directions, and do not be surprised if you find that your horse will turn quite easily and naturally in one direction and has a very hard time going the other way; this is quite normal and will be corrected by schooling, and practicing the turns a little more often to the difficult side.

Once your horse will turn easily on the haunches from walk, practice the turn from the halt. The difficulties here are an increased tendency on the part of the horse to turn on the centre, letting the haunches fall out, and the lack of activity of the hind legs, i.e., pivoting on the inside hind. If you have taught the horse what you want by teaching the turn first from walk, however, you will have much less trouble getting your horse to turn correctly on the haunches from the halt.

Haunches-in (also called Travers and head to the wall)

Haunches-in, like shoulder-in, is best developed from the circle. Start the movement in walk, but as soon as the horse understands what you want him to do, practice haunches in mainly in trot, to keep the active, forward movement going more easily.

Walk your horse round a circle to the left. At a point just where his forehand reaches the track, push him away along the track in haunches-in. Ultimately, the horse should be bent equally throughout his length in the direction in which he is going, in this case, to the left, and he moves obliquely sideways along the track.

At first glance, this movement seems to be the same as shoulder-in but with the horse placed differently in the school, however, this is not so. In shoulder-in the inside rein, acting as an indirect rein of opposition to the quarters, actually helps in the moving of the quarters along the track because the horse is bent AWAY from the direction of travel. In haunches-in the use of the inside rein, which is necessary to maintain the bend, actually works against what you are trying to achieve with the quarters.

At the start of haunches-in we ask for only a very slight bend, or even none at all. It is much more important that the horse maintains rhythm and forward movement than that he is correctly bent, which can come later, provided you do not obstruct his forward movement now. When starting to teach haunches-in, therefore, be careful not to increase the contact with the inside rein when the horse leaves the circle and proceeds along the tangent in haunches-in. In fact, slightly lighten the feel on the inside rein, and bring the outside hand a little closer to the shoulder and slightly lengthen the outside rein by yielding with your fingers.

The leg aids are fairly obvious, the outside leg is drawn back behind the girth to push the quarters in, and the inside leg remains at the girth to assist in achieving the correct bend and to produce forward impulsion.

The haunches-in prepares the horse for the half-pass, which is the ultimate aim of all the lateral suppling exercises, and it exercises the same muscles and joints as in the shoulder-in, but in a completely different combination. The horse does find it a more difficult exercise than shoulder-in, and the bend is a less natural one. Your horse will probably try to avoid bending his neck and body in the direction he is going and may straighten it, or even bend it the other way. At the beginning, the bend, and the degree of angle from the track are very important compared with the necessity of keeping up the regular rhythm, the impulsion and the same length of stride, which can only be achieved with a very light hand. Gradually, as the horse becomes stronger and more supple, you will be able to correct the bend and increase the angle from the wall until it is correct.

Haunches-out (also called Renvers, and tail to the wall)

The movement 'haunches-out' is exactly the same as the movement 'haunches-in'. The only difference is the position of the horse relative to the sides of the school. This is not so with the shoulder-in, for instance, which is always called shoulder-in no matter where it is performed in the school.

Producing haunches-out, of course, necessitates riding the horse along the inside track, or bringing the shoulders in preparatory to starting the movement, in order to have room for the quarters to be moved out onto the track. Everything already said about haunches-in applies equally to the movement haunches-out. Haunches-out has the advantage of being a more logical straightening exercise for the young horse who has a tendency to align his outside up with the wall of the school and thus travel constantly with the quarters slightly in, since all horses are narrower through the shoulders than through the hips.

Refinements of haunches-in and haunches-out

In both these exercises the horse moves obliquely sideways, being throughout his whole length in the direction of the movement. 'Oblique' refers to the angle of the horse's body with the line of his progress. In early training this angle should be kept very small indeed or the impulsion will not be maintained. The bigger the angle, the more difficult it is to keep up the free forward movement.

The finished horse should be able to perform haunches-in at an angle of 45°, but even the finished horse would be better to concentrate on impulsion, during practice, and only work at an angle of about 30°. The angle of 45° is equivalent to the bend required of the horse in performing a perfect volte of one horse's length (circle of 10 feet diameter) and this is exceedingly difficult even for a fully trained horse, so you will understand why, at first, you must keep the angle very slight indeed.

When flexion is demanded of the head and neck, in the direction of the movement, it must always be slight. Flexion is only correct if the head carriage itself is correct, and if the horse's head remains vertical. Too often the flexion is attempted by a sideways and upwards pull of the leading rein which results in the head being tilted. This tilted head is a very serious fault, more serious than insufficient flexion, no flexion, or even more serious than wrong flexion. It is also an exceedingly difficult fault to eradicate. The best way to avoid this head tilting is to be very, very light with your hands.

Haunches-in and haunches-out on the circle

Once you and your horse have mastered haunches-in and haunches-out on straight lines, the same exercises may be practiced on the circle. At first, the circle should be large. The haunches out on the circle is practiced a great deal by the Spanish Riding School and is a very useful exercise for a horse of the build of the Lippizaner, but it does have a tendency to hollow the horse's back and put the weight onto the forehand because the quarters have to travel further than the shoulders when the horse is asked to perform haunches-out on the circle, and the quarters are not as easily mobile sideways as the shoulders. For general purpose schooling it is probably better to stick to haunches-in on the circle. Because the hindquarters have to travel a shorter distance than the shoulders at haunches-in on the circle, the result of this exercise is to make the forelegs take longer strides than the hindlegs. Because the hindlegs and forelegs move in time, the result of the exercise is to extend the front legs and markedly flex the hindlegs, and bring the horse's weight more onto his haunches.

This exercise must be done with great care to see that the flexion does not change, that the relative rhythm and the relative length of the strides of the forehand and the quarters remains constant and that the position of the horse on the two concentric circles remains constant. This demands great control and lightness. As you achieve this, you may practice the exercise on smaller and smaller circles, which will culminate, gradually ,in the pirouette.

After the horse has mastered the exercises in walk, they may be practiced in all the gaits; that is, walk, trot, and canter. On the circle, haunches-out should only be performed in walk, however, but haunches-in may be practiced at all gaits.

Half-pass

Lateral work is absolutely essential for the development of active and free forward movement in the horse. Free forward movement is the result of correct and active use of the hind legs, thrusting deep under the body in a state of flexion, and the muscles of the loins and hindquarters being strong and well developed are able to drive the horse forwards. Correct lateral work is the means by which we achieve the strengthening of the muscles and joints of the hind leg, the quarters, and the loins.

In shoulder-in, haunches-in and haunches-out we ask the horse to move obliquely sideways. In half-pass we ask him to move obliquely forwards, gaining as much ground forwards as he does to the side, and stepping well under his body with his outside hind leg so that it crosses over in front of the inside hind leg. The forelegs, also, must cross, so half-pass helps develop mobility and suppleness of the shoulders as well as the hind quarters. The forehand should always slightly lead the quarters in half-pass, and the whole horse, from nose to tail, should be bent very slightly towards the direction in which he is going. That is, in right half pass, the horse is bent to the right, around the rider's inside (or right) leg.

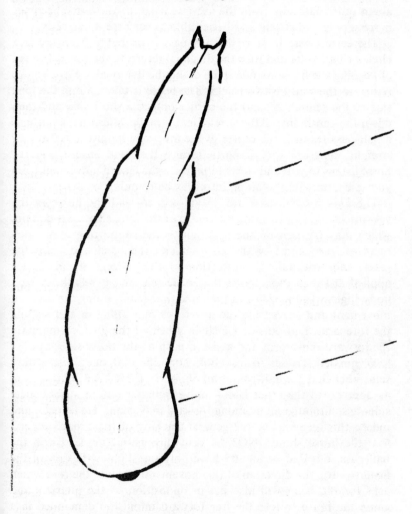

Half-pass

Many books, and for that matter, many trainers, suggest starting half-pass with the horse bent the wrong way and gradually achieving the correct bend. I do not agree with this philosophy. It seems to me to be unnecessary to teach the horse something that we don't want him to do. When starting half-pass for the very first time, I simply ask the horse to stay straight, to keep the head straight in front of him, and then, gradually, we develop the correct bend, which comes about quite naturally from the exercise itself, as the horse becomes more supple and strong and better able to perform it correctly.

The easiest way to start the half-pass is probably from the half circle or half volte and then the diagonal return to the track. Instead of keeping the horse on one track along the diagonal, we ask him to return to the wall on two tracks. The horse is taken along the long side of the school, around the corner onto the short side and then down the centre line. After a few steps straight ahead he is put into a half-pass towards the centre of the long side he just left. The few straight steps are very important since they will ensure that the horse listens to you and starts to perform the lateral movement from your aids, not simply falling into it as he rounds the corner.

The aids for half-pass are, inside rein to lead the horse in the new direction, i.e., towards the centre of the long side; outside rein, which may be used on the neck and is the supporting rein which regulates the degree of the position and the bend and helps the inside rein maintain the direction of the movement; inside leg applied at the girth supports the inside rein and bends the horse's body slightly to the inside at the same time maintaining the forward movement and preventing the quarters from falling in and leading the forehand; and outside leg slightly behind the girth to maintain the forward movement and assist in pushing the horse sideways.

Wynmalen stresses in his book *Dressage* that one must always remember that the half-pass is an obliquely FORWARD movement as opposed to the other lateral movements which are all obliquely sideways, although maintaining forward movement. He teaches, and indeed this seems to be the general teaching of the French school, that the horse should NOT be bent throughout his length in the half-pass, but that he should have only the slightest flexion of the head towarts the direction of the movement, because the rein which asks for the bend will also act in opposition to the quarters and cause the horse to lose the free forward impulsion demanded in a good half-pass. Podhajski, on the other hand, states the more classical, or perhaps Germanic, teaching, that the horse must be bent, and that the bend is created more by the inside leg than the inside rein.

I have found, in practice, that the necessary forward impulsion is more easily produced in half-pass if the horse is kept completely straight at first. Once the horse is more practiced in the movement, the bend, which should be very slight indeed, is easily produced by the use of the inside leg. Too much dependence on the outside leg in achieving half-pass has a definite tendency to push the quarters in advance of the forehand, a very bad fault, and I therefore use Wynmalen's suggestion of gradually training the horse to produce half-pass more from the rein aids and from the seat than from the drawn back outside leg, which leaves me both legs free to produce the vital forward movement.

Half-pass, like all lateral movements, should be taught in walk initially, until the horse understands what is required of him, but should generally be practiced in trot, and later in canter, because it is undoubtedly much easier to maintain forward movement in trot than it is in walk. The regular rhythm of the horse's steps must be kept and the contact on the bit should remain the same as when the horse is on a straight line. In practicing the half-pass it is advisable to put the forehand well in advance of the quarters at first and sacrifice some of the crossing of the outside legs, in order to avoid the development of the very serious fault of the haunches leading.

Counter changes of hand

Half-pass may be practiced as described above, from the centre line back to the wall, or from the wall to the quarter or centre lines, or, ultimately, across the diagonal. A very useful exercise at half-pass is the counter-change of hand, which is simply a short half-pass to one direction, followed by three or four steps on a straight line, followed by a short half-pass to the opposite direction. The horse should be made to go straight for one horse's length before changing direction to avoid the possibility of him throwing himself into the new lateral movement with the quarters leading, which remains a tendency until the horse has perfected his balance and suppleness. Counter changes of hand, or short half-passes in opposite directions, are very useful in the training of young horses who are apt to hurry their steps.

As with all lateral movements, and indeed with all schooling, make haste slowly. Remember to be satisfied with a very little at first and do not ask for too much all at once. Half-passes, particularly, if they are repeated and repeated during one schooling session, will tend to lose rhythm and forward movement. Remember always that any exercise, if it is to be of value, must be performed at the right moment and in the right way.

More Advanced Work in Canter

I have already mentioned the danger of neglecting the walk during the training of your young horse. The canter, also, may have a tendency to become a neglected gait.

It is easy to become so involved in perfecting the work you are doing with your horse in trot that you may not leave yourself sufficient time, nor your horse sufficient energy, to bring along his work in canter at the same time. Bear in mind that all three gaits, walk, trot and canter, are of equal importance and that a certan amount of work in all gaits is necessary if your horse is to progress satisfactorily in his training.

You will probably have noticed, and particularly if your horse does not have a very naturally impulsive trot, that right from the stage of early lungeing, if you work him in canter and then return to the trot, the trot is improved. At first, of course, the work in canter should be mainly outside and should consist of a good, active, long striding, swinging canter. The horse will be in a comparatively long shape and moving freely forward on straight lines or very large circles. This long, swinging, unhampered gait will be perfectly natural to a horse who has been ridden mainly outside and who has, perhaps, hunted, and will do a great deal towards the suppling of the horse's spine. However, for the 'school canter'—the gait we must now develop to continue the dressage training of our horse— the pace of this outdoor canter will be much too fast. The problem which faces us, therefore, is to collect the canter without in any way spoiling its natural three beat rhythm or inhibiting the deep swing under the body of the hind legs.

Lightness

The canter can easily be slowed down, of course, by the use of the reins, but if you resort to the reins to slow the horse in any gait, the results are disastrous to the purity of that gait and to the freedom and elasticity of the horse. The wonderful, soft, swinging of his back, which is our goal, is lost.

So many riders seem to think that a tight and quite strong feel on the reins is not only unavoidable but also good. It is not. On the contrary, it is bad, quite unnecessary, and can be easily avoided. We should think seriously to ourselves about what we truly want from the schooled horse. Do we not want him to be light, balanced and fluent in his movements? If we want a 'light' horse it is essential that we build confidence between the horse and ourselves, and that we never apply any but the lightest aid. Lightness, balance and fluency are the result of confidence and impulsion. Lightness is not something which we obtain later in the horse's training, it is something which must happen right from the very beginning. That is why we use only the lightest possible aid and we insist that the horse 'carries himself' in all his work and does not 'lean' on the reins.

So often a rider says to me 'but my horse is leaning on the reins'. It does not seem to occur to them that it is absolutely impossible for the horse to 'lean on the reins' unless the rider, in turn, allows this to happen and supports the horse with his hand. EVERY horse can go lightly—indeed, is longing to go lightly. Even a horse accustomed to having the rider pulling on the rein most of the time can be taught how to go lightly, with a contact of just the weight of the rein and perhaps the strength of two fingers, in a matter of a few minutes if ridden by a sensitive and tactful rider. Once you have experienced a truly light and balanced horse you could never wish for your horse to be any other way. Teachers or trainers who fail to make their horses light, or their students capable of riding with sensitivity and lightness, have much to answer for, in perpetuating the idea that the rider must hang on to the horse's head. I have elaborated on this subject in the chapter headed *On the bit* but here I would like to add that the horse is not slowed down by the reins, he is slowed down by the rider's seat.

Control through the seat

Try this simple experiment for yourself. Remember that when your horse is walking, your seat is following the movement by freedom of movement in your lower back. Your hand is 'allowing' the horse to walk by moving slightly back and forth following the movements of the horse's head and neck, the rein is very lightly taut. If you wish to slow the walk down, simply cease following quite so much with

your seat and think in the slower rhythm. Don't do anything with
the rein but play very very slightly with the fingers of the inside hand.
The horse is enormously sensitive to the weight and exact position
of the rider. Provided you are sitting on your seat bones, with the
thigh and calf only lightly in contact with the horse without any
grip or clinging, the legs simply 'breathing' with the horse, he will
respond almost instantly to the slowing action of your seat following
him less.

This experiment is even more dramatically apparent in the sitting
trot. Establish a very slow trot at first, with the horse 'round', that
is, in the correct shape of a horse, head down, back round, not hollow.
Sit erect, deep and do not grip. Keep your hands low and very still
with only the lightest contact, just playing with the fingers of the
inside hand, and if the horse is stiff, allowing with the fingers of the
outside hand. Now, slow the trot down even more by ceasing to
follow with your seat and still just playing with your fingers. So
strong is the slight backward displacement of the shoulders and the
cessation of the following action of the seat, that you will have to use
a little light intermittent pressure of the inside calf in order to keep
up the impulsion and ensure that the horse continues in trot.

To lengthen the stride, yield with your fingers and allow your seat
to follow more freely by completely loosening the small of your back.
Do not drive with your lower leg, simply keep it there in light contact
with the horse. Squeezing, gripping and driving with the lower leg
will cause contraction of the horse's muscles and loss of freedom
of the forward swing of the hind legs under the body and the forward
reach of the shoulders. If, at first, the horse does not respond to the
increased action of your back, use the whip, lightly, once, to help
him to understand that this will henceforth be your aid for more
impulsion. Trot in the lengthened stride, keeping the same rhythm
that you had in the slow trot, for ten or twelve strides, then bring
the horse back to the slow trot with a much shortened stride but
again the exact same rhythm, simply by the use of the seat—cease
following the horse, bring your shoulders back slightly. Never grip
or you will come out of the saddle and bounce. At first, the shortened
trot, although slower, will not be a collected trot because it will lack
the impulsion necessary for a collected gait, but once correct rhythm
and miles per hour have been established, impulsion can be gradually
increased by correct use of the back and correct application of the
lower leg. So many people confuse impulsion with speed and the
two have nothing at all to do with each other.

The gaits—canter and gallop and Aids for canter

To return to the canter; it is important to understand that the canter is a pace of three time. When cantering with the off-fore leading, the horse's feet come to the ground in the following sequence: first the near hind, beat one, then the off hind and near fore together, beat two, then the off fore, beat three. The third beat is followed by a moment of suspension known as the fourth or silent time of canter, and then the sequence starts all over again.

In nature the canter is a fairly collected gait. The horse at liberty canters with his head and neck raised and his balance is consequently moved backwards, more towards the quarters. The drive from the hind legs is delivered, as in all collected gaits, when the hindlegs are more or less vertical under the horse. The effect is therefore more lifting than driving forward. This fact explains the easy balance of the canter and the comparative lack of speed.

The gallop is quite different. It is a pace of four time in which the sequence of footfalls in the gallop on the right lead is as follows: first the near hind, beat one, then the off hind, beat two, then the near fore, beat three, then the off fore, beat four. The fourth beat is followed by a moment of suspension and then the sequence begins all over again. The gallop is much faster than the canter and the extra speed is developed by the fact that the hindlegs are well behind the vertical when they deliver their drive. The horse's balance is carried well forward and the three time gait no longer suits this altered balance. (It is worth mentioning that in reading translations of classical works on horsemanship, or even modern works written by Europeans whose native tongue is not English, the canter will often be seen referred to as 'the gallop'. This can be very confusing if the reader is unaware that the author is, in fact, speaking about the canter and the translator has simply used the French word for canter instead of translating it.)

From the point of view of dressage, the canter must always remain a pure gait with three distinct beats. If four beats develop, which unfortunately happens all too often, it is a lazy gait and the horse will not be able to get his hind legs well under him and raise the forehand. Four beat canter lacks impulsion and is a totally faulty gait usually acquired through incorrect schooling.

The generally accepted aids for canter are the diagonal aids—outside leg slightly back, inside leg at the girth, and inside rein. However, these aids do have a disadvantage. Horses are not by nature straight at canter. They all carry the quarters to the inside. The diagonal aids, with the outside leg back, tend to encourage this crookedness by placing the quarters to the inside even more. This certainly ensures that the horse will strike off on the correct lead, but it makes the job of keeping the horse straight at canter well nigh impossible. Straightness didn't matter to the old masters, the more they went sideways the more they liked it, but then they didn't practice the flying changes. It is only when the horse is absolutely and perfectly straight that the flying changes in canter can be performed correctly. So, from our point of view, straightness in canter does matter a great deal.

Provided your horse is collected and has sufficient impulsion the canter strike off can be achieved with very little, or no, use of the lower leg at all. Ride your horse in collected walk on a large circle. Start to think the rhythm of canter in your head—one-two-three, one-two-three, but keep your body erect, and still. Then give the aids to canter, but precede the leg aid by a touch of the inside rein. At first, use your voice as well. For example, touch the rein and say 'And' then leave quite a long moment between this preliminary warning and the application of your legs, both together just behind the girth at which precise moment you say 'Canter'. The time lapse between the preliminary rein aid and the legs will enable you to avoid any restraining action of the rein and this is a very important consideration indeed. Do all this very smoothly, with a very quiet voice. You will find that soon you do not need the lower leg at all, simply the pressure of the inside seat bone, which will automatically be carried slightly in advance of the outside seat bone due to the fact that both the inside hind and the inside front legs of the horse are carried in advance of the outside legs in canter. Ultimately, the sensitive rider can obtain canter without the use of either leg, or with the use of both or just one of them to enable him to keep the horse perfectly straight.

Teaching the horse to strike off in this way, with the preliminary warning signal of the rein, is of enormous help when we come to the flying changes of lead.

Beware of exciting the horse with this work. Absolute calmness on the part of the rider and the horse are essential. To help ensure calmness, work at first on the large circle and canter only a few strides before bringing the horse back to a quiet walk on a long rein. Then pick up the rein, collect the walk, and start again. The exercise must, of course, be practiced equally to both directions, and can be practiced outside on straight lines, but don't canter first right lead, then left, then right, and so on, at least, not in any regular pattern, or the horse will quickly start anticipating.

I want to stress again that it is very difficult to do this work and maintain calmness in the horse and yet it is vital that you do so. Working at canter can so easily upset and spoil a horse. Use only the very lightest and most careful aids and NEVER any force. It is very good to use the voice throughout these exercises until the horse is completely relaxed and confident in performing them.

Slowing the canter

The exercise described above of cantering for only a short stretch and then bringing the horse back to a walk very calmly and quietly without any pulling on the reins, will, itself, help you to slow his canter. Your horse will very quickly understand that you only intend to canter a short distance and he will therefore begin to slow down the pace in anticipation of your aid to walk. Done in this way, with no restraint on the reins, you will be able to maintain the natural, free, long stride of your horse with nothing forced in his position and no danger of losing the true three beats of canter.

Once your horse has slowed his own canter sufficiently, you can begin to use this slow canter for longer and longer distances. If anything surprising or upsetting happens, which makes your horse speed up, for instance, if a bird flies up and he shies, do not give in to the temptation to slow him down with the reins, but instead bring him back to a walk and continue to walk on a loose rein until he is completely settled, then start your canter again.

This work at canter is not going to come right all in a day. If good results are to be achieved you must be prepared to have a great deal of patience, but the end results are enormously worthwhile. First of all, you will quite soon find that you can control your horse, even when he is excited, with the very lightest touch of the rein, and secondly, this work at canter is very suppling for the horse's back and will therefore help to improve his suppleness at trot.

Transitions into canter

Most of the lower level tests these days, both in England and the United States, ask for the canter from trot. The reasoning behind this is logical—that if novice riders ask green horses to canter from walk they may do considerable harm to the horse's schooling because they don't understand what is collection, nor how much collection and impulsion are necessary for the strike off. It is felt, therefore, that they are less likely to interfere with the free forward movement of the horse if they make the strike off from trot.

There is one big disadvantage to striking off into canter from the trot, and that is that if the horse is used to going on into canter from trot, it may become very difficult to get him to extend his trot —he will always be wanting to canter when you drive him forwards more vigorously. In view of the fact that, if you wish to compete with your horse, you must make a certain number of transitions into canter from trot, I recommend that you practice transitions both from trot and from walk in your schooling. It is much easier to strike off from the walk, really, provided you know what you are doing, because you have more time to balance and place your horse and you will have much more feel of exactly what the horse is doing.

Transitions from walk to canter, on either leg, are, in any case, an essential part of the preparation of the horse for the flying changes. The transitions must be calm, smooth and fluent and the horse must have absolute confidence. If he gets excited it is a sign that you are not being sufficiently tactful with your aids. You must remain calm and quiet yourself and never do anything to upset your horse. Be content with reasonable progress and don't be upset if your horse occasionally strikes off on the wrong leg, above all, never get rough. Remember that, since you are trying to get him to strike off correctly from an ever finer aid, so, occasionally, he is going to misunderstand. You and he will progress together towards even more lightness so long as you remain calm and reasonable.

Transitions from canter to walk

Obviously, the downward transitions from canter to walk are closely bound up with the work we have just been considering, of transitions from walk into canter. Until this stage in your horse's training I have suggested that you allow his canter to subside gradually into walk, through a few intermediary steps of trot, by simply allowing his impulsion, and therefore his collection, to subside. Provided your horse has reached the stage where he will accept your leg aids as the means of producing and maintaining impulsion without increasing his speed, you will be able to slow the canter very easily by the use of your back, as described under the heading 'control through the seat', while still maintaining his impulsion with the use of your lower leg.

As your horse becomes more aware of your wishes, he will begin to offer more fluent and briefer transitions of his own accord. At that time you may make use of a more positive rein aid, always very light however, and always supported by your legs. In fact, you will very quickly find that your horse becomes much more attentive and offers you calm and balanced transitions into canter from walk and into walk from canter, maintaining his impulsion and collection, with very little more than the use of your seat and the slight backward displacement of your weight. This presupposes that your horse is cantering slowly, with impulsion, and on the bit, in the correct 'shape'. If he is still at the stage where he cannot maintain the correct shape in a slow, impulsive, canter, he is not ready for this work.

More transitions—halt, canter, halt

Once you have mastered the strike off into canter from collected walk, the strike off from the halt is not difficult to achieve, provided your horse is able to stand perfectly square and in a state of collection. The preparatory rein aid is, of course, even more useful in the canter start from halt because it allows you to indicate to the horse which lead he is to strike off on, without any retarding action of the rein at the moment of departure.

The strike off from halt must be performed without any intermediary steps. That is, the horse must lift himself from the halt directly into a true canter stride. He does this on either lead, quite easily, by using the stationary hind leg as the first 'beat' of canter and lifting the diagonal (for right lead, the left front and right hind) which constitutes the second beat, followed immediately by the leading foreleg.

The aids are exactly the same as those used for a strike off from walk. Do not ask the horse to strike off from halt until he has thoroughly understood the exercise of strike off from walk.

The transition into halt from canter should be performed exactly the same as the transition from canter to walk, and you allow your horse only to round out the stride and bring his legs squarely under him. In other words, if you stop all forward motion as the leading foreleg strikes the ground the horse can stop very easily from canter at that moment, but he will not be square and therefore the halt will be incorrect. If, instead, you stop the canter at the moment when the leading foreleg touches the ground and then allow the diagonally opposite hind leg to take one step in walk and the front leg on the same side to take one walk step, the horse will be standing perfectly square in a correct and collected halt.

It is only through practicing these movements with your horse that you and he will gain the necessary experience and mutual feel which will enable you to perform them, so don't be afraid to practice the exercises. Canter collected around your school, turn up the centre line, or up the quarter line, make a halt, sometimes in the centre, sometimes three-quarters of the way up the school. Strike off on the same lead, turn into the track at the top of the school; half way down the long side, turn across the school. Halt on the centre. Strike off in canter on the opposite lead, turn in the opposite direction when you reach the track, and so on.

At the start of this work, remember that it is extremely demanding for both yourself and your horse. The horse is asked to keep himself physically in a state of collection, and mentally in a state of complete concentration, and the rider must also be in a state of complete, relaxed concentration. So give yourself and your horse frequent rests on a long rein at walk.

Half pass in canter

Half pass in canter is no more difficult than half pass at trot or at walk. It is a valuable suppling exercise and once your horse can canter sufficiently slowly in a 'school canter' maintaining impulsion and with a certain degree of collection, you can introduce half pass at canter. I usually start by bringing the horse down the long side in collected canter, turning up the centre and from the quarter marker asking him to move away in a half pass back to the track at the far quarter marker. On reaching the track come back to walk.

It is never a good idea to practice an exercise in one place in the school consistently, so remember that you can also half pass inwards from the quarter marker on the long side towards the centre. Start out by asking only for three or four steps in half pass and then straighten your horse and continue on a straight line to the end of the school. Ultimately you will be able to maintain the half pass all the way across the school, but, as always, progress should be made slowly and remember not to ask too much too soon. It is very important that the horse performs the half pass correctly, with the correct bend to the direction in which he is going, and leading slightly with the forehand. Maintaining perfect balance, suppleness, lightness, and correct bend will take considerable practice. One of the most common mistakes is insufficient use of the INSIDE leg which results in the horse 'popping' or 'falling onto' the leading shoulder. See the chapter on *Work on two tracks*.

You need not, of course, confine your work at half pass to the school. Take advantage of any lane or path with good going when you are out hacking to practice your half passing, either in trot or canter—or indeed, in walk. If your horse has difficulty maintaining sufficient impulsion, practice the movement going towards home so that all your problems of forward movement are solved for you by the horse's own natural desire.

The counter-canter

This is the stage in your horse's training where you can usefully begin work at counter-canter. This exercise will ensure that your horse never changes his leading leg in canter except upon his rider's specific command. It is absolutely indispensible, of course, as a preparation for the flying changes that the horse should understand this. Most horses will change leads in the air of their own accord when they change direction—this is the natural thing for them to do to maintain their balance in the easiest way, so work at counter-canter is to some extent asking an unnatural thing from the horse, but it is vital that he learns how never to change leads until commanded.

Counter-canter is also a very good suppling exercise, simply because it asks the horse to use his muscles in a combination that he would not normally use and to find his balance in performing a movement which he would not normally use.

Counter-canter is also known as false canter, and not to be confused with 'cantering disunited' which means with one lead in front and the opposite lead behind and should be so totally impossible for you on your horse at this stage that there is no need to say any more about.

In counter-canter we ask the horse to canter on a curve, or ultimately, a circle, with the outside leg leading instead of the inside leg leading as would be natural for him. This is also a disciplining exercise where we confirm that the horse is acting only in obedience to his rider and giving up his own natural wishes and to some extent his natural balance in favour of an artificial balance which we teach him.

Since your horse is, by now, perfectly used to obeying you, his
rider, it is not a difficult exercise to teach him. However, it does
require tact and careful explanation. The horse will probably, at
first, change his lead anyway, even though you are maintaining your
aids for canter right whilst curving to the left. If he does so, do not
punish him. After all, a little later in his training you are going to
ask him for flying changes and if you punish him now for giving
them to you, he may remember that punishment and be unwilling
to lay himself open to it again. If the horse changes leads without
being asked, simply return to walk, walk for a few minutes until he
is completely calm, and repeat the exercise.

I like to start counter canter by asking for a long shallow loop
on the long side of the school. For example, in left lead canter, come
around the short end of the arena in an anti-clockwise direction and
in a fairly collected canter. Start down the long side and then begin
to loop inwards towards the centre, and complete a smooth, shallow
loop returning to the track before the corner. Working outside, if
you have a large field, can be a great help. Try this exercise outside.
Start around the field in a clockwise direction. On a long straight
line, ask for a strike off on the near fore (left or outside lead). Sit
still and quiet and keep your horse rather strongly on the aids,
particularly maintaining the rein aid which gives the flexion to the
left. Without changing the aids for canter, use the right rein to
produce a curve to the right. Remember always to turn your head
and look in the direction you wish to go. Develop this exercise until
the curves become more marked and eventually form a broad, shallow serpentine. Do not change leads during the serpentine, so that
your horse will be cantering alternately in a true canter and in a
counter-canter. Later on, develop the serpentines into large circles
and figures of eight without changes of lead.

These exercises in counter-canter are difficult and will take a great
deal of time and patience and practice to perfect. Do not be in a
hurry and do not punish your horse for any misunderstanding of
your explanations. Remain calm yourself and make sure that your
horse remains perfectly calm and relaxed throughout the work.

It is as well to understand that to gain the full benefit of the
suppling exercises in counter-canter, the horse must remain flexed
to the leading leg, but must be able to allow his body to conform
to the track of the movement. This requires considerable suppleness.
Flexion means a relaxation of the horse's jaw to the action of the
rein and a 'tendency' in that direction. It does not mean a bend

of the horse's neck in the direction of the rein aid. This distinction is particularly important if you are to gain the full benefits of the counter-canter. Your horse should ultimately be able to bend around your inside leg, whilst maintaining the counter-canter and a flexion of the mouth to the opposite direction, that of the canter lead. This is demanding a very great deal and will only be achieved after much time, patience and hard work. Like everything else in the training of the horse, it cannot be achieved by force—the horse, when ready, will give it to you freely.

25 *More about Show Jumping*

Combinations

As you continue your jumping training you will find it useful to work through combinations of varying distances to improve your horse's agility, judgement and balance and ultimately, your control over the shortening and lengthening of his stride.

It is important to keep the obstacles very small at first. Start out using two fences, say a single rail at about two feet followed by a small parallel or oxer type fence about 2 feet 6 ins. high and 2 feet wide with 18 feet between them. Trot the first fence and allow one canter stride between the fences. As time goes on, add a third fence, still very small, but use as much variety as possible, and place the third fence about 24 feet from the second. When the horse is calm and confident over three fences in a row, add a fourth fence and later even a fifth of varying types and at varying distances. Take plenty of time and never add more fences if the horse is excited or fearful.

After completing the exercise the horse should be brought quietly to a walk, on a straight line following the last fence, and not allowed to turn sharply to one side or the other in an attempt to rejoin his companions.

When the horse becomes competent at these small fences with varying distances, raise the height inch by inch, and increase the spreads a very little at a time. At the same time, continue to vary distances between the fences; for example, you will normally have 24 ft to 26 ft between two obstacles of 3 ft 6 ins. to be jumped in canter, but when the horse is competent, change this distance sometimes and put only 21 ft between the fences. Follow this combination with a low in-and-out, say 2 ft in height, with 12 ft between the two fences. This will cause the horse to jump without taking a stride—he will 'bounce' over the fences.

It is much practice over very small fences which finally brings confidence and calmness to the horse and makes him into a 'great' jumper over any course.

Value of lungeing over fences

You may continue lungeing your young horse over fences with advantage, even when you begin this work over combinations, especially if he is only a four or five year old and you will save much strain and jar to his legs by eliminating your weight during his jumping practice. When you lunge over in and outs be careful to have the fences ranged along a solid fence or wall, on the side away from you, and the standards near you must have a pole with one end resting on the ground and the other on the top of the standard, so that the lunge rein will slip easily up the pole without catching on the standard or the jump (*see illustration in chapter* 9).

Combinations naturally discourage rushing, but if you do have a problem with the horse rushing, try long-reining over the fences. The advantage is that with the two reins you have much more control over the horse, both on the approach and after he has landed. One word of warning, do not try to long-rein over fences until you are very good at it on the flat and have had lots of practice with an experienced horse. It looks much easier than it is, and it is very important that you have the reins completely loose as the horse is actually jumping.

The rider's position—control of the engine

The rider's position on the approach, over the fence, and on landing, is a matter of much controversy. I do not believe that the rider who leans forward with a hollow back and his seat out of the saddle on the approach to a fence is capable of preventing the horse from refusing or running out if he tries and it is the prevalence of this position, particularly in hunter classes in the United States, which, in my opinion, leads to the endless refusals one sees in hunter classes, even over very small fences, under 4 ft. In order to be in control of the horse the rider must control his engine—the hindquarters. The hindquarters, as we have seen in previous chapters, can only be effectively controlled by the rider's seat and legs, not by his hands. Therefore, it follows that if the rider leans forward and, by hollowing his loins, removes his seat from the saddle, he is relinquishing this essential control. The same principle obviously holds on the landing side of the fence.

On the approach to the fence the rider should sit still. His seatbones should be in the saddle and his back relaxed and straight, his upper body only slightly inclined forward. His legs should be in contact with the horse's sides, which is impossible if the thigh is gripping, and the knee pressed in. The legs and seat should be used actively on the approach and during the take-off. By 'using' the legs and seat I mean applying a series of rhythmic squeezes to the horse's sides with the calf of the leg and a strong forward drive with the seat bones, to ensure that the horse is truly and constantly 'forward' throughout the approach. The reins, which should be held only very loosely during early training, should be kept very lightly taut once the horse has reached the stage of jumping through combinations in canter. The rider's fingers should be relaxed and ready to allow the reins to slip, over the top of the fence.

On take-off, but not before, the rider bends forward from the waist and hips and allows his hands to move forward following the movement of the horse's head, in much the same way that a child on a rocking horse will naturally lean forward as the front of the horse rises up towards him. The rider's seat will be raised out of the saddle by the action of the horse's shoulders and back as he levers his forehand off the ground, and then, as the horse thrusts upward from his hindlegs, the rider's seat will come close to the saddle again, so that it is easy for him to sit softly back into his saddle on the landing side of the fence, once again upright and with a light contact, ready to take the next obstacle, turn, change pace or stop as required. On no account should the rider stiffen his back or try to stand up in the stirrups during a jump as this will put him out of balance with the horse, and also out of control of the horse's 'engine'.

The rider will find it much easier to maintain this correct position if he shortens the stirrups three or four holes, or more, from his dressage length.

Negotiating turns

When jumping a series of fences with changes of direction between them, the turns are of the utmost importance. The horse should be steadied or checked, as necessary, coming into the turn and, if necessary, the leading leg changed (through trot on a green horse, by means of a flying change on an experienced one). The turn itself is accomplished mainly with the outside leg and rein. If you use the inside or opening rein you will turn the horse's head only and his hindquarters will fall out. He will no longer be straight and if the next fence is of any size or difficulty he will be incapable of negotiating it correctly simply because he is physically unprepared.

If your horse shows signs of rushing into his fences, as many keen horses will do, even after they have had considerable training and have gained quite a lot of confidence in their own ability, do not try to slow him down by pulling on the reins. If you pull, he will stiffen and pull against you so that your efforts will have little effect. The horse needs to feel that his head and neck are free to be used as a balancer during his jump, so be certain to keep the reins only lightly taut on the approach with your fingers and hands following rather than restraining the horse. If he needs collecting or steadying before the jump and your reins are only very lightly taut, just the slightest resistance with your fingers should be sufficient to achieve the desired result, provided you are sitting still and relaxed in the correct position. If the horse still rushes, correct the fault after the fence, not in front of it. Immediately on landing, bring the horse to a walk (without any roughness) and walk calmly for several minutes. Then try the fence again. Incidentally, if he is prone to rushing, jump small in and outs in preference to single fences as this will make him think more and he will be less likely to run. Sometimes vary your routine and circle the horse in front of the fence, approaching quite close to it and on the approach line but then circling away several times before actually asking him to jump the fence. Again, on landing, bring the horse quietly to a walk and walk on a loose rein completely relaxed for a while before doing any more jumping.

Patience will eventually bring calmness and calmness is essential in a jumper who must be free to use his judgement and agility to negotiate larger and more difficult courses.

Jumping narrow fences

Until the horse is really confident your jumps will be low and inviting with a wide face and preferably with wings, but now it is time to start jumping small obstacles without wings, and also to reduce the size of the fence across its face and to practice over narrow fences. In fact, it makes little difference to the horse whether the fence is ten feet across its face or only three, but it makes a great deal of difference to the rider. At first, of course, you must keep your narrow fence very small, and you may find it helpful to place wings about four feet away from each side of it. You approach in a quiet, active trot. Sit well down on your seat bones with your legs relaxed, but on the horse and active. On no account hollow your back. Pay particular attention to the corner before the fence and approach the fence completely straight with your weight just behind your horse. Stay sitting on your seat bones until the moment when he takes off and then bend forward. Remember to slip the reins as the horse jumps to avoid any possibility of catching him in the mouth if you get slightly left behind.

Jumping narrow fences helps with the straightness of the horse and is an important part of his training as well as being a very good way to determine if you can co-ordinate the use of your seat and hands. Jump only from a trot until you are confident and practiced in the technique and then you can try it from canter, provided your horse is calm and relaxed also.

Practice riding all your fences in this same way, regardless of the width of the face of the fence, and you will be assured of a straight approach and a better, more athletic and confident jump from your horse.

Jumping in a horse show

When you start taking your horse to small schooling shows you will be taking another big step forward in his training. It is one thing for a horse to perform well at home, but it is quite another thing for him to travel to a strange place and then, amid all the excitement and confusion which surround any show, to perform with equal confidence. Small schooling shows are the proper place to begin your horse's show education. Be sure only to enter him in classes where the jumps will be about six inches lower than those you have been working over at home. Actually height is less of a difficulty for the horse than most riders think, but staying well within your accustomed height range will ensure that the rider remains calm and confident at all times and therefore that the horse performs well.

A plan of the course should be displayed in or near the collecting ring at least half an hour before any jumping class and this plan will give you a great deal of valuable information. It will tell you the class number and name and the rules under which the class is to be judged. It will show you the distance of the course and the speed (usually in metres per minute but sometimes in yards per minute) at which the course is to be ridden, and also the time allowed. The plan of the course will also list the fences to be used in the jump-off or jump-offs, the distance of the jump-off course, the speed and the time allowed. The course plan also, of course, shows you the position of the start and finish lines and the position of each fence in the course numbered on the right hand side of the take-off side of each fence, in the order they are to be jumped.

From this plan you can work out an approximate route to follow. Combination fences will be drawn separately and numbered a, b, or c, in addition to the fence number. There may be directional arrows shown on the plan and these are simply to help eliminate any doubt about the direction in which you must jump each fence. Sometimes a solid line may be drawn on the plan with arrows indicating direction incorporated in it. In this case, you must follow the line exactly or you will be disqualified for taking the wrong course.

Having learnt the way round the course thoroughly from the plan and digested all the information, you will not waste any time when, as should happen before each jumping class, competitors are allowed into the arena to inspect the course on foot.

Walk the course on your feet before the beginning of each class. Follow the track your horse will take and make a mental note of the angles required for the turn between each fence as well as stepping the distance in combinations so that you will be prepared to lengthen or shorten the stride as required. In schooling shows all courses should be flowing with no sharp turns or trick fences placed so that they must be taken directly out of a corner, but later on in your show jumping career your ability to bring your horse correctly round a difficult corner keeping him balanced and calm may make the difference between winning and losing a big competition.

It goes without saying that you must have the course completely memorised before trying to ride it and also, of course, you must plan the best approach to each fence, deciding whether to take a wide turn, perhaps passing around another fence, or to cut a corner here or there in a speed competition and thus gain valuable seconds. During your first year of competition you will stick to the small shows, but soon the time will come to try something more testing and the confidence and control you build up in those early shows will stand you in good stead for the whole of your horse's competitive life.

Jumping spread fences

A word about spread fences may be appropriate here. Many riders think that because there is a little spread on a fence they must somehow jump it differently. This is not really true when we consider spreads of anything up to about five feet. With bigger spreads than that you do make a slight difference in the way you approach.

With the smaller spreads of two, three and four feet, simply ride the fence as if it were an upright. Your horse's natural parabola will easily take you over such small spreads cleanly. Larger spreads will not concern you during the first year of your horse's showing, but when the time comes and you are jumping bigger courses and often big combinations with spreads of six feet or more on oxers or parallels you must remember that more impulsion and more precision are required to clear these spreads faultlessly. The impulsion is created by the rider's seat and legs, the precision by the rider's brain and his ability to shorten and lengthen the horse's stride. If a fence has a big spread on it you must not let your horse take off too far away. In fact, your correct take-off platform is considerably narrowed in just the same way as it is when the fences begin to get high—that is, above 5 feet.

Jumping upright fences

If you have to jump a high fence which is also completely straight up, you can add width and so give yourself a better chance of jumping faultlessly by approaching the fence diagonally instead of head on.

Take off zones

The take-off platform (the area of ground in front of the fence from which the horse must jump the fence if he is to clear it correctly) for a 3 foot fence is anywhere from three feet out from the base of fence to nine feet away. When the fence is higher the take-off platform gets much smaller—for example, if the fence is 6 feet high the take off platform is only six inches wide. Jumping higher fences requires very great precision and the ability to lengthen and shorten the stride and maintain the impulsion of the horse throughout the approach, take-off, landing and departure from each fence.

Preparing for your first round

Before taking your horse into the arena to compete in a jumping competition you must, of course, warm him up. The length of warm up will depend to some extent on the individual horse. Usually about half an hour is enough, and certainly a good part of this time should be spent on a long rein allowing the horse to stretch and limber up his muscles. I usually walk, trot and canter on a long rein for ten minutes or more before asking anything much from my horse and then pick up the reins and begin to ask him to put himself together and think about the job in hand. Some lateral work in walk and trot, halts, rein back, starts and stops from canter, all help to put his hindquarters under him and prepare him for the job at hand. I like to make quite sure the hores is limber and responsive at canter before any jumping and I often use increases and decreases on the circle to achieve this. Six to eight strides in a shortened canter followed by eight strides or so at a lengthened canter, followed by another shortening, and so on. Then you will want to take a few practice fences. Start out with three or four fences at trot—quite small ones, just to get the hocks under your horse and prepare him for the jumping effort you are going to demand of him. Then three or four fences in canter—if possible two different fences, one an upright and one a spread.

Every horse varies in how much jumping he needs before he goes into the ring but it is as well to remember that jumping tires a horse quite quickly and although you must ensure he is well limbered up and prepared for the job at hand, you do not want to wear him out before the competition begins.

Try to time your warm up so that you do not have too much time to stand around before you enter the ring for the first round, and keep the horse active, alert, and in a short frame, trotting and halting, or with a little lateral work in walk before you enter the ring. Once in the arena, concentrate totally on what you are doing and follow the track you have prepared in your mind.

The jump-off

Before the jump-off you will probably want to jump another couple of fences to prepare the horse for the added height, but again, be careful not to overdo it. Only experience with each individual horse will tell you exactly how much warm-up is enough for that horse.

By far the most important part of your body in all your riding is your head, or rather, your brain. It is just the same whether you are about to enter the show jumping arena, the dressage arena or set off on a gruelling cross-country course, you must know exactly what you want from your horse and concentrate fully on what you are doing so that you forge that all-important mental link with him and communicate your determination and superiority to him with calmness and complete confidence.

26 *Flying Changes of Lead in Canter*

As your training progresses and you and your horse have perfected the simple change of lead and the canter to halt to canter transitions and work in counter canter described in chapter 24 you will be ready to start working on the change of lead in the air. This flying change is a completely natural movement to the horse, but it is certainly not easy to obtain correct changes on demand. The difficulties lie with the rider rather than the horse, since it is not easy to apply the aids for the change without hindering the horse's execution of the movement.

How the horse changes

The horse actually makes the change of leading leg during the fourth, or silent beat of the canter when all his legs are off the ground for a brief instant. In this fraction of a second he must reverse the relative position of all his legs. If he is cantering on the off fore, the first step is taken by the near hind, then the off hind and near foreleg together and lastly the leading leg, the off fore; followed immediately by a moment of suspension when all four feet are off the ground. If there is no change of lead, this sequence continues, but after a change it alters and the off hind comes to the ground first, followed by the near hind and off fore together, and then the near fore and finally the moment of suspension.

The canter lead is determined by the hindleg which initiates the sequence. If the near hind strikes the ground first the canter will be on the right lead, and if the off hind is the first beat, the canter is on the left lead.

For the flying change to be correct, the horse must reverse the relative position of his legs whilst all four feet are off the ground in the silent phase of the canter. The new hind leg must come cleanly through and bend well under the horse, there must be no speeding up or slowing down of his pace, and the rhythm of the canter must remain exactly the same. There should be no jolting felt in the saddle —in fact, a perfect change is very hard to feel from the saddle because it is completely smooth and comfortable to ride. There should be no swinging of the horse from one direction to another, indeed he must remain completely straight, calm, relaxed and impulsive throughout the change.

Preliminary work

Before you even start thinking about the possibility of practicing flying changes, all the canter work described in the chapter headed *More advanced work in canter*, (*ch.* 24) must be absolutely confirmed. Your horse must be able to strike off in canter from a collected walk and a collected halt, on either lead, canter two or three strides and come immediately back to a collected, impulsive walk or halt. He must be able to remain perfectly straight in the transitions and have achieved considerable collection, using his hocks energetically and remaining very light in hand. In other words, he must be in perfect balance, and able to maintain considerable collection without being held on too short a rein, which will interfere with the execution of the change.

Counter-canter is an essential preparation for the work in flying changes. You should be able to maintain counter-canter on a twenty metre circle, with the horse correctly bent around the circle and remaining very light in your hand, balanced, relaxed and active. He must not change his rhythm of canter at all and should move easily from the counter-canter circle into a circle on the true lead, so that you are performing figures of eight with no change of lead. During these exercises in counter-canter you may find it helpful to think of keeping your outside shoulder back. That is, the outside shoulder of the canter, in other words, cantering with the off fore leading you should keep your left shoulder back.

This positioning of the upper body will ensure that you keep your outside (in this case, left) leg on the horse and slightly increase the use of the outside, left, rein. This combination of aids has the effect of 'closing' the left side of the horse and 'opening' the right side and therefore ensuring that he maintains the right lead. Neither the body position nor the leg or rein aid should be exaggerated, and ultimately you will need no more than the use of your seat bones to maintain the canter and to produce the flying changes, but at the outset you must make sure that your aids are completely clear to the horse and that they are as easy as possible for him to understand.

Timing the aid

The biggest difficulty in the flying change is for the rider to be able
to give the aid for the change at the correct moment. The aid must
be given a certain time ahead of the required movement by the horse,
but exactly how long a time lapse is necessary is very hard to say.
Probably the best moment to apply the aid is during the second beat
of the canter, when the horse has the leading foreleg extended ready
to strike the ground and is supported on the other three legs. If you
practice a little, this moment is not hard to determine from the
saddle.

First changes

To make things as easy as possible for the horse at first, ask for your
change during a change of direction. Concentrate hard on the rhythm
of the canter, counting the one-two-three beat to yourself. Slightly
exaggerate the aids for the canter you are in, that is, if you are
cantering on the left lead and you are going to make a change to the
right lead, keep your right shoulder back, right leg on, and slightly
more feel on the right rein until the second beat of the stride before
you wish to make the change, and then simply and definitely reverse
your aids. Do not swing your horse, it is unnecessary, looks bad,
and will probably lead to disunited changes. Make one change only
and walk the horse for a while on a loose rein. If you fail to make the
change correctly, walk anyway, and when the horse is completely
calm, try again.

In most cases the horse will make the change with no problem at
all. Be satisfied with only a few successful changes each day. At first,
perhaps only three or four, and gradually, as time goes on, ask for
more changes, but never very many, and keep up the practice of
walking for a while after each change for several weeks. This will
ensure that your horse remains calm and calmness is absolutely
essential for work on flying changes.

Difficulties and their cures

If your horse did not make the change correctly when you asked
for it, walk for a while and then try again. On no account get excited
or rough or punish the horse. Several things can happen to interfere

with the purity of the change. Perhaps your horse is putting in one stride of trot instead of going directly into the flying change. This could mean that you are using too much hand and that your rein aid is retarding the change. Try accelerating into and through the change. The change is actually easier for the horse on a longer stride, and although, ultimately, he must neither speed up nor slow down his pace when changing, initially you may find that slight acceleration can help this problem.

Disunited change

Another common difficulty is that the horse may change in front but not behind. This is unlikely to happen if the work at canter departs from walk and halt and counter canter has been correctly done, but if it does, it probably happens because you failed to apply the new aid sufficiently clearly or at the correct moment. Do not be satisfied with a change that is in front only. Walk calmly for a while and then repeat the exercise, taking greater care over the application of the aids, and, if necessary, using a touch of the whip behind your leg, until you get it right.

Delayed changes

If you ask for a change and the horse does not change leads on the next stride but gives you a delayed response in the following stride, the problem is likely to be that you failed to warn the horse that the aid was coming. Once your horse is trained to the degree that you are ready for flying changes, you, the rider, will actually be doing very little indeed. You put the horse in canter with a certain leg leading and he will stay lightly in balance, at that canter, with the same amount or impulsion without any further interference from you. You may have to regulate his impulsion, or keep him straight, but your role is a passive one. However, the horse is not then able to execute totally unexpected commands for flying changes.

You must draw your horse's attention to the fact that you are going to ask for something new, and you do this by accentuating the aids for the movement which he is doing, a stride or two before asking for the new movement, the flying change. As your training progresses the length of time necessary for your warning will be reduced until it is given just a moment before you ask for the change. This warning must be given to the horse with no suddenness and no roughness. You must never surprise your horse, whatever you do. But you can use this moment of warning to increase his impulsion, or speed, or both if you feel it necessary, before you ask for the change of lead.

Changing on straight lines

When your horse performs the changes during a change of direction with ease, confidence and maintaining his balance, rhythm and impulsion, you can ask for changes on long straight lines. Be careful not to ask for changes in the same place in the arena, or your horse will quickly start to anticipate the changes. If he does start to anticipate them, despite your care, go back to work on counter canter and do not try another change until he is completely settled and listening to you again.

Changes on the straight can be practiced outside, where there is plenty of room for a long, straight canter, and no risk of anticipation by the horse. Canter quietly along, bring the horse onto the aids by applying the aids for the canter you are in, make your change and then walk. Walking after each change is very important as it ensures that the horse stays completely relaxed.

Importance of calm

Do not be in a hurry to perform more than one change at a time. Be quite certain that you can perform the changes on straight lines, both outside and in the school, smoothly, easily and fluently, and with absolute precision on your demand. Then work on large circles in counter-canter and make the changes inward to the true canter, and follow this with work on straight lines in true canter and change outwards into counter-canter. When all this work is confirmed and the horse remains perfectly calm through the change continue in canter a little longer after the change and ask for another change about twenty or thirty strides further on and then walk.

If you attempt to hurry the work in changes and continue repeating the lesson, you will not succeed. The whole basis of the work is purity of the changes, that they should be performed on demand, and that the horse should remain calm. This takes a great deal of time and patience and the horse must necessarily spend a good part of the lesson, which itself should not be more than fifteen minutes, at difficult concentrated work, in a relaxed walk.

Sequence changes

Once your changes are accurate and calm every twenty strides or so, you will find no difficulty in reducing the interval between changes to eight or ten strides. At this point you are ready to begin work on the sequence changes, say every six strides to start with. It is a good plan to spend some time first perfecting your control in counter-canter and also in canter departs from walk, making sure that your horse is absolutely straight, controlled and calm. Start by asking for a collected walk on a large circle, and a canter depart on the true lead, six strides of collected canter and a transition to collected walk. Six strides of collected walk are followed by a strike off in counter-canter on the circle, and after six or seven strides make another transition to walk. Be careful to vary the number of strides between transitions or the horse will start to anticipate.

Repeat the lesson a few times in each direction. Then work in canter, changing every five, six or seven strides, but never in the same sequence and never more than a few changes consecutively, followed by some walking. You will soon find that you can change every four strides with no problem at all.

Beyond this, the reduction of the strides between the changes becomes more difficult. Changing every three strides is best approached as follows. Canter with the off fore leading, and a considerable amount of impulsion. Change to the near fore leading, do three strides exactly, change back to the off fore leading and walk. Repeat several times in the exact same sequence so that the horse is practicing the change from near fore to off fore only. It is less confusing and your progress will be quicker if you work in this way. Practice the change from near fore to off fore for two or three days and when it is completely controlled, reverse the exercise and practice the change from off fore to near fore in the same way, for a day or two.

Only then do you join the two exercises together and canter three strides on the off fore, change to three strides on the near fore, change back to the off fore, and make a transition into walk. Next you must practice the same exercise in reverse, starting out on the near fore.

When you have mastered changes every three strides you must make quite sure that the horse is not simply changing as a matter of routine, so you must work for some days in changes at will, some after three strides, some after four or five strides.

Changes every two strides are worked out in the same way, but it is as well to understand that this work on changes at very short intervals is difficult and demands very precisely timed aids and a tremendous degree of understanding between horse and rider. To teach the work correctly the rider needs considerable experience, judgement and tact to avoid any trace of excitement or confusion in the horse. But it is also immensely interesting and rewarding work and brings a great sense of achievement when successfully completed.

Preparing for Horse Trials and Three-day Events

Perhaps the most exciting, the most sporting and the most rewarding of all horse sports is, as the French call it, the 'Concours Complet'— Eventing, which covers everything from the one day Horse Trials to the three-day Event. It will take at least a year's experience in Horse Trials and One-day Events before your horse is ready to compete in a Three-day Event, but the basic principles of preparation are the same whether you and your horse are newcomers to the sport or whether you are seasoned competitors.

Conditioning

A young horse who has never been fit before takes much longer to bring into hard conditions than an older horse who was fit the previous season and has been let down and allowed to rest for a few weeks. Conditioning depends on the correct balance of diet, exercise and work, and grooming.

Feeding

There are probably as many different opinions about correct diet as there are horse trainers, but the majority agree on the basic principles. All forage given to horses must be the very highest quality obtainable. It must be clean, free from dust or mould, wholesome and sweet smelling. I prefer to feed my horses timothy hay which has been undersown with clover. A timothy and clover mix seems to me to give the horse the best of everything, and I feed it more or less free choice during the early stages of getting the horse fit. As I increase the grain ration so I reduce the hay somewhat, until, after about twelve weeks the horse is getting about 15 or 16 lbs. of grain and 10 to 12 lbs. of hay daily. At this point he would be fit and hard and ready to go in any one-day event.

It is important to remember that each horse is an individual and what suits one will not necessarily be the best thing for another. You must watch your horse very carefully and discover from experience what diet suits him best. But if you are intending to Event him, then he must be getting sufficient grain to give him the necessary energy and not too much hay, as too much bulk in his system will affect his wind.

Keeping a feed chart on each horse is a good way to keep track of exactly what he is eating. All food should be carefully measured or weighed and, if possible, fed in several small feeds each day rather than in two large ones. Below is a sample of what your feed chart might look like.

Feed Chart

Twelve weeks prior to competition (same for four weeks—then gradually increase grain, decrease hay)

7 a.m.	5 lbs. hay
	3 lbs. rolled oats
12 noon	3 lbs. rolled oats
5 p.m.	10 lbs. hay
	3 lbs. rolled oats
	1½ lbs. broad bran
	1 cup soymeal
	2 tablespoons wheat germ oil
	¾ pint cold water
8 p.m.	3 lbs. rolled oats

Before his rest day each week the horse should have a bran mash and on rest day he should have less grain and, if hay is less than 10 lbs. he should have more hay. As training progresses the main difference in the feed chart is a reduction in the hay until the horse is down to 10 to 12 lbs. daily, depending on his size, and an increase in the oats until you are feeding 3 lbs. at 7 a.m., 4 lbs. at noon and 5 lbs. at 5 p.m. and 8 p.m.

Importance of water

The horse needs a constant supply of clean, fresh water and free access to salt. Some horses need to be fed iodized salt in their feed. If your horse has a tendency to dehydration, consider feeding electrolites (obtainable from your veterinarian) daily for several weeks before a competition. The only time water should be withheld from your horse is just after exercise, until he has completely cooled down, and for about an hour or two before a gruelling competition. Some people withhold water, and food, from the horse for very much longer periods before a race or an event, but I have found that most horses, if they are accustomed to having water constantly available, will not drink too deeply at any time but will tend to take just a few mouthfuls. Certainly you do not want to fill your horse's system with a large drink of water just before asking him to gallop round a cross country course, any more than you would want to drink a large quantity yourself, but a few swallows, especially if it is very hot, will certainly not hurt him. The same thing holds good for his hay. You do not want him to fill his system up with bulk just before asking him to gallop and jump, but a small quantity of hay in the early morning will help to prepare his digestive tract for his grain feed and will help to keep a nervous horse calm by giving him something to do in his stall or on the journey to the showground.

On the day of a competition you will have to consider the times that you are in competition when thinking about feeding your horse. The early morning feed will not be affected, but if you ride your dressage test at 8.30 a.m. and your cross country at 11 a.m. you may not show jump until 4 p.m. or 5 p.m. and there is plenty of time in between for your horse to have a drink and a small feed (about 3 lbs. oats), just as you, yourself, will want a small drink and a sandwich but certainly not a full meal until your exertions are over.

Exercise and work

Just as important as correct feeding is the proper balance of work and exercise, and good grooming. Your daily work as described in previous chapters will, to some extent, get your horse pretty fit.

However, when you start to think about entering a competition, you will need to increase the amount of 'road work', which need not be done on the roads but includes long steady trotting up and down hills and, three or four weeks before your competition, you will introduce some galloping—about half to three quarters of a mile at half speed, twice a week. This is to improve the horse's wind and surprisingly enough the horse should NOT be galloped more than twice a week and then not at full speed. The best system I have found is to include two gallops, half a mile or so, at half speed in the fourth week before an event. Two gallops in the third week before an event, one of them slightly shorter and followed by half a mile at three quarter speed. The same during the following week which is two weeks before the event, but lengthening the distance to about 1 miles at half speed. Then, the week before the event which is probably on that Saturday, I give the horse a one mile gallop on Tuesday at three quarter speed and I don't gallop him again until the event.

The work the horse does each day should include at least half an hour of dressage and usually I find I work a little longer than that. I like to do my road work early in the morning and I build up from just about half an hour, twelve weeks before a competition, to one hour eight weeks before, and one and a quarter hours six weeks before. Four weeks before the event my road work will be up to nearly two hours, but this will include my gallops on two days a week and plenty of time at a long, loose rein walk afterwards for the horse to recover, and it will also include my jumping practice one day a week. Usually I will get the horse out twice a day. If I do the road work early in the morning I will do three quarters of an hour of dressage in the afternoon. However you organize your exercise and work, be sure to leave your horse plenty of time, at the same time each day, when he can lie down and rest completely.

Importance of rest day

Every horse needs one day a week as a rest day. This does not mean he must stand in his stall all day and, in fact, it is much better for him if you can turn him out in a paddock to graze for an hour or so on his day off. I try to get my horses some fresh green grass every day. If possible they are turned out for half an hour and if that is not possible they are led out after work on a halter and allowed to nibble the grass for ten minutes. I also feed two or three carrots a day to make sure the horses get 'something succulent every day'.

Keep an exercise chart

It is not always easy to remember exactly what you did each day
with each horse, especially if you have several to get fit at the same
time, and you may find it worthwhile to keep a chart of your training
programme and check it off each day after you work each horse.
Below is a sample of an idea for what a chart might look like for
one week for one horse, but if you are getting fit for a specific event
you will find it more useful to start your chart eight to twelve weeks
beforehand and include all twelve weeks on one big chart pinned in
your feed room or tack room or even on the loose box door.

Training programme: Week one (fill in the dates)

Day	Dressage	Road work	Jumping	Galloping
Mon.	$\frac{1}{2}$ hour	$\frac{1}{2}$ hour	none	none
Tue.	$\frac{1}{2}$ hour	$\frac{1}{2}$ hour	none	none
Wed.	$\frac{1}{2}$ hour	$\frac{1}{2}$ hour	none	none
Thur.	$\frac{1}{2}$ hour	$\frac{1}{2}$ hour	none	none
Fri.	$\frac{1}{2}$ hour	$\frac{1}{2}$ hour	none	none
Sat.	$\frac{1}{2}$ hour	$\frac{1}{2}$ hour	none	none
Sun.	Rest Day			

During the first week of getting fit the chart isn't very exciting,
but when you reach week nine or ten you will really appreciate the
readily available information. Some people prefer to make up charts
they can check off instead of filling in. The important thing is that you
should keep a record of the work you do with each horse each day.

Grooming

Good and thorough grooming every single day is essential to get
your horse fit and into top condition. Before you ride, his feet should
be picked out and oiled (I use a mixture of pine tar and vegetable
oil) and he should be quickly brushed over to make him look neat
and tidy before he goes out. His real grooming takes place on his
return from work when his pores are open and he gains most
benefit from it. It will last approximately three quarters of an hour.
   Start by cleaning him off with the dandy brush or rubber curry
and then use the body brush in long sweeping strokes with some

weight behind them over his whole body, paying particular attention to the muscles on his neck, shoulder, and quarters. Use your hay wisp or the folded stable rubber to 'wisp' or 'bang' these large areas of muscles. Use a forceful, sweeping, glancing motion along the line of the neck, on the shoulders and on the top of the quarters. Do not use this 'wisping' or 'banging' on any other part of the body, certainly not on his loins or rib cage.

If it is hot and the horse was sweating after his work it is a good plan to sponge or wash him down and then walk him dry before grooming. The horse will appreciate this bathing and provided the weather is suitable it will not harm him. Keep him out of the wind after you have washed him and walk him dry in a sheltered place.

After using your body brush and wisp or stable rubber, sponge the horse's eyes, nose, mouth, sheath and dock area, pick out his feet and oil them on the wall and the soles. Once a week the sheath should be gently cleaned out with warm, soapy water and thoroughly rinsed. This is to remove the accumulation of secretions of dead skin and surface cells which are called smegma and which, if allowed to build up inside the sheath, can be a source of irritation to the horse. Most horses do not object at all to having the sheath washed but it is advisable to cross-tie the horse to prevent him from moving in circles. If you are quiet and gentle in your approach you are unlikely to encounter any problems. Remember the importance of thorough rinsing as soap residues can be as irritating as smegma to the horse.

Cross country jumping

If your training has been directed towards this most fascinating of horse sports, eventing, you will certainly have spent a long time thinking about the cross country and how best to prepare for it. Even if you are lucky and have plenty of country to ride in with some good natural obstacles to jump, you will certainly be the exception rather than the rule if you have plenty of good cross country jumps to practice over, and I honestly do not believe that you need them in order to compete successfully. If your dressage is right, and your show jumping is right, and your horse and you are in good condition mentally and physically, the cross country phase should cause you no difficulty.

No one can possibly introduce their horse to all the different jumps used in cross country, but everyone can ensure that his horse is calm, confident, obedient and going freely forward, straight. After that, you need to understand a few basic rules about cross country jumping, and then you need to gain experience for yourself and your horse by entering in small one day horse trials or hunter trials and going hunting if you can. You must build up gradually to the bigger competitions.

When you ask your horse to gallop across country and also to negotiate large, fixed obstacles, on differing terrain, you have to understand that you, the rider, are there to help the horse and not simply as a passenger. It is not good enough to allow the horse to gallop as fast as he likes and just hope that you can point him at the fence in time. This is where training comes in. Even when galloping, your horse should be listening to you and you should be able to 'rate' him by closing your fingers on the reins, and bring him back to you a little bit so that you can balance him for turns and fences. It is also your job to try to protect your horse from harm on the course, and since prevention is better than cure I suggest fitting a running martingale and over-reach and brushing boots as a matter of course any time you are planning to gallop, jump or take your horse cross country.

Galloping position

When you are actually riding a cross-country course in competition you will spend most of the time in the galloping position—that is, with your seat out of the saddle and your upper body inclined forward. In this position your weight causes the least possible inconvenience to the horse. You 'hold' the horse with your back and your thigh and not with your hands so that although you should have a good contact, with a nice steady feel in each hand, you should never have to 'pull'. As you approach a fence, when you are still about sixty yards away, sit down into your saddle and check your horse slightly. Your check will be more, or less, depending on the obstacle you are approaching. For an upright fence at maximum height you check more than you do for an oxer or a triangular shaped fence with a good ground line well out in front of it. Then, with your seat bones in the saddle, you ride the fence, using your judgement about length of stride, pace, angle of approach and so on, exactly as you would in show jumping. After the fence, you raise your seat out of the saddle and resume the galloping position, unless the fence is one of a series of closely related obstacles, or one element of a combination.

Jumping downhill and uphill

If a fence is placed on a downhill slope your horse's stride will lengthen into the fence. If it is on an uphill slope, his stride will shorten and you may need more drive than you would for the same fence placed on the flat. In both cases you have to get your body a little more forward than for a fence on the flat in order to be 'with your horse'. If you do get left behind, simply slip the reins out through your fingers and pick them up on the landing side.

Water

Jumping into water, slow down. It is often a good idea to trot a fence into the water, but in any case, slow down. On no account gallop madly at it. Hitting the water is like hitting a solid wall for the horse's legs and if you come in too fast they will suffer considerably at the least, and at worst the horse may somersault. Make sure you walk through the water and test the bottom when you are walking the course. Do not be content to prod it with a stick—get into it and paddle about.

Drop fences and step fences

Jumping drop fences is much like jumping a fence on a downhill slope. You steady the horse and take the fence slower than you would take a similar sized fence on the flat. If you come in too fast there is a danger of the horse falling on the landing side due to too much impetus which he is then unable to control. Jumping uphill over a series of steps or banks, you will need a little more drive than usual to overcome the shortening effect on the stride of the uphill grade.

Combinations

Combination fences on the cross-country are handled in much the same way as combination fences show jumping. Remember, however, that if it is a 'galloping' course, that is, if you are on rolling grassland, perhaps coming downhill, your horse's stride will be considerably longer than in the show ring. In fact, on cross-country, you are asking your horse to gallop on and stand off his fences and jump flatter than in show jumping. A big horse moving on a little may need 30 to 36 feet for a one stride in-and-out on the cross-country, though he may be able to handle a 24 ft. in-and-out perfectly well on the shorter stride he will use in the show jumping. When walking your course be particularly careful to step out the distances between elements of combinations so that you will be forewarned and able to slow the horse down and shorten his stride in plenty of time if you have a short combination.

Coffin fences, those with a post and rails on a downhill slope, one stride, then a ditch, then an uphill slope with another post and rails one stride later, often cause difficulties on cross-country courses. Remember not to look down into the ditch yourself on the approach. Even though the first element is on a downhill slope you may have to ride into it quite strongly because the horse may suddenly see the ditch and start to put on the brakes. Make sure that your horse is well in front of your leg before approaching the fence, but try not to take your hand off the reins to hit him just as you are approaching. This is usually a mistake as the horse ducks out sideways. You are really better advised to sit well down on your seatbone and drive the horse forward than to try using your whip as encouragement. The real problem with coffin fences is that riders fear them. This fear transmits itself immediately to the horse who decides to stay well away.

Vision

Another thing to consider when you are jumping a cross-country course is that if you are asking your horse to jump from a sunny field, over a gate, or any fence, into a wood, you are asking him virtually to jump blind. His eyes take much longer than yours to adjust to the light and therefore, jumping from the light into the dark area of the trees is harder for him than jumping out from the wood into a bright field.

Timing

Timing, how fast your horse is actually going, is a very important part of eventing. It is something that you learn with experience, though you can get a fair idea of your horse's speed by measuring a distance where you normally do your galloping and then timing yourself over the measured half-mile or mile. This may help you to get a general understanding of your horse's pace but it won't be an accurate guide, because of course, in the cross-country you are going to have fences to negotiate, steep downhill slides and steep uphill climbs and so on.

Riding in the competition

When you are taking part in a competition you must make yourself a time schedule and know exactly how many minutes you have to cover a certain distance. Keep a close check on yourself, but, if you find you are falling behind the time you had hoped to make, you will have to use your discretion about whether to push on faster. There is a danger of going too fast early in the course and having no horse left for the final mile or so. But it is equally frustrating to finish with no jumping faults and to lose the competition by having too many time faults. The time allowed is deliberately fairly fast and equivalent to the old 'maximum bonus' times. It is as well not to push your horse too much in the early competitions, let him gallop at his own speed, knowing you can rate him easily for his fences and that he will finish with plenty in hand. This way he will not suffer much strain from the competitions and he will thoroughly enjoy himself. This is important for his future attitude—he must enjoy his work if he is to do it really wholeheartedly and well.

Riding in a one-day horse trial

If the competition you have been preparing for is a one-day event you should arrive at the show grounds in plenty of time to walk the cross-country course again, even if you walked it the day before. If your dressage time is very early, you may want to walk the course after riding your dressage test, but in any case, be sure to walk the course again sometime before you have to ride it.

The first time you walk the cross-country course you must assess each fence individually. Decide exactly how you plan to jump it and then stick to your plan. It is permissible to jump across a fence at an angle, if this will help you in your approach to the next fence and does not make the fence impossibly wide or big. However, with a young, green, horse, choose the easiest possible approach to every fence and do not ask any big questions.

The second time you walk the course pay particular attention to the overall pattern of the course and be riding it in your imagination.

At least one of the times you walk the course you should go alone. You will concentrate much better if you are not chatting with your friends. When you come to ride the course, ride with calm determination, remembering that the first fence is always the most difficult and requires the most riding, but that even easy fences can present problems and your total concentration is required until the moment you pass through the finish flags.

If you do have a refusal do not get upset. Stay calm and try the fence again. You must know if closely related fences are marked as two or three separate jumps or as a combination. Combinations are marked 1a, 1b and 1c or 1a and 1b. Fences marked consecutively, 1, 2, 3, are not combinations even if they are close together. At each individual fence you are allowed two refusals before elimination, and you may not retake an obstacle already jumped to get at one you refused. At combinations you are allowed only two refusals total before elimination. In the case of combinations, if you refuse at, say, the third element, you may decide whether to retake the whole obstacle or just to retake the element you refused. Be particularly careful about which way you turn inside a combination if you have a refusal at one part. You may not cross your tracks or it is counted as a circle, which is another refusal. If you do not understand this fully be sure to ask someone to explain to you exactly which way you may and may not turn inside a combination in the event of a refusal. The Technical Delegate is usually available to answer such questions for you.

The show jumping course

After walking the cross-country course, walk the show jumping course and assess it carefully. Decide how best to ride each fence and notice the turns, and how tight they are. Pace the combinations and make sure you know the course thoroughly and can ride it in your imagination, just as you should be able to do with the cross-country.

Sequence of phases

One-day events may be organised in two ways—the dressage and show jumping phases may precede the cross-country, or you may ride dressage, cross-country, then show jumping, in the traditional order of the three-day event. As soon as you arrive on the grounds, go to

the Secretary's office and collect your number cloth and a programme and ask about any possible changes in timing. Then, if your
dressage test is early, prepare yourself and your horse for the
dressage phase.

It is a good plan to lunge your horse for ten minutes or so as close
as possible to the arena where you will be riding your dressage test.
This will calm the horse and allow him to take a good look at its
surroundings before having to compete. To do this you may have
to arrive at the show ground extra early, before the dressage begins,
but, with an excitable horse, this is often worthwhile.

Ride on your horse for at least half an hour before your dressage
test is due to begin and if you know that your horse needs more than
half an hour to get suppled up and listening to you then prepare for
a little bit longer. However, bear in mind that it is going to be a very
long day for you and your horse, and half, to three-quarters of an
hour warm-up should be plenty for anyone.

After riding your dressage test you should have plenty of time to
walk the cross-country course for the second time before preparing
for the second phase, whether it is show jumping or cross-country.

It is correct to have your horse's mane plaited for the dressage
test and for the show jumping, but not for the cross country, so if
the phases are arranged with the show jumping before the cross-
country, you will be able to undo his mane before riding. If your
cross-country comes before the show jumping, however, do not
attempt to undo the mane and re-plait it. There simply will not be
time. Ride the cross-country with it plaited.

With all the hard work and training and preparation behind you,
enjoy your day at the competition. Remain cool, calm and determined, and make sure that your horse enjoys his day too. Of course,
you will have butterflies or 'nerves' before entering each phase, but
they will go away as soon as you start to ride and this 'strung-up'
feeling, which will certainly be shared by your horse, will only add
to the terrific 'high' you will get on satisfactorily completing the
three tests of the competition, mounted on your own horse, which
you have trained yourself.

Index

Weaning, 27
Wheat germ oil, 204
Whip, the, 44
Whips, use and abuse of, 129–131

Winging, 16
Wynmalen, Henry, 6, 155, 166, 174

Yearling, the, 28